THE OFFICIAL REGULATIONS TO THE QUALIFYING AND AWARDING OF THE CAMPAIGN STARS AND MEDALS INSTITUTED FOR THE 1939-45 WAR

For Service on
Land, Sea, Air & Approved Civilian Categories

The Naval & Military Press Ltd

Published by

The Naval & Military Press Ltd
Unit 5 Riverside, Brambleside
Bellbrook Industrial Estate
Uckfield, East Sussex
TN22 1QQ England

Tel: +44 (0)1825 749494

www.naval-military-press.com
www.nmarchive.com

In reprinting in facsimile from the original, any imperfections are inevitably reproduced and the quality may fall short of modern type and cartographic standards.

CONTENTS

SECTION I
GENERAL

	Para
Preamble	1
Classes eligible for awards	2
Order of wearing and description of ribbons and emblems ...	3
Concurrent service and aggregation of service	4
Land—Definitions of qualifying service on land	5
Air—Definitions of qualifying airborne service	6
Sea—Definitions of qualifying seagoing service	7
Combined operations personnel	8
Civilians—special approved categories	9
Special awards	10
Service in Enemy or Enemy occupied or in Neutral Territories ...	11
Allied and other Foreign Nationals	12
Disqualification and Forfeiture	13

SECTION II
QUALIFICATIONS FOR CAMPAIGN STARS AND MEDALS

1939-45 Star 14
    Qualifying land areas (180 days) 14
    Qualifying special areas (one day) 15
    Airborne service 16
    Clasp (Air Crew) 17
    Sea going service 18
    Qualifying sea areas 19

Atlantic Star 20
    Sea going service 20
    Qualifying areas 21
    Airborne service 22
    Clasps (alternative awards) 23

Air Crew Europe Star 24
    Airborne service 24
    Clasps (alternative awards) 25

Africa Star 26
    Land service 26
    Qualifying land areas 27
    Airborne service 28
    Sea going service 29
    Clasps 30
        8th Army
        1st Army
        18th Army Group H.Q.
        Limitation of awards
        North Africa 1942-43 for R.A.F.
        North Africa 1942-43 for Seagoing service

	Para
Pacific Star	31
Land service	31
Qualifying land areas	32
Airborne service	33
Sea going service	34
Qualifying sea areas	35
Clasp (alternative award)	36
Burma Star	37
Land service	37
Qualifying land areas	38
Airborne service	39
Sea going service	40
Qualifying sea areas	41
Clasp (alternative award)	42
Italy Star	43
Land service	43
Qualifying land areas	44
Airborne service	45
Sea going service	46
Qualifying sea areas	47
France and Germany Star	48
Land service	48
Qualifying land areas	49
Airborne service	50
Seagoing service	51
Qualifying sea areas	52
Clasp (alternative award)	53
Defence Medal	54
Army qualifications	54
Threatened, etc., areas	55
Local Commissions and recruitment overseas	56
Home Guard	57
Approved civilian categories	58
Colonial Empire and mandated territories	59
Foreign subjects	60
Civilians, United Kingdom	61
Civil Defence Organizations overseas	62
Emblem	63
War Medal 1939-45	64
Army qualifications	64
Approved civilian categories	65
Sea going service	66
Foreign subjects	67
Emblem	68
India Service Medal 1939-45	69
Qualifications for award	69
Indian army categories	70
Ineligible categories	71
Method of application	72

SECTION III
ADMINISTRATION

Serving personnel
Forms of application	73
Instructions for claiming Campaign Stars	74
Instructions for claiming Defence Medal	75
Instructions for claiming India Service Medal, 1939-45	76
Procedure for verification and disposal of forms	77
Transfers and re-enlistments	78

Non-effectives
Forms of application	79
Instructions for claiming Campaign Stars	80
Instructions for claiming the Defence Medal	81
Deceased personnel	82

Commonwealth Forces ... 83
Colonial and Local Military Forces ... 84
Colonial Police ... 85

Specially approved civilian categories—
Instructions for claiming campaign stars	86
Procedure for verification and disposal of forms	87
Instructions for claiming the Defence Medal	88
Instructions for claiming the War Medal, 1939-45	89
Deceased personnel	90

Home Guard—
Instructions for claiming the Defence Medal	91
Disposal of claim forms	92
Deceased personnel	93

Foreign subjects (Military)—
Forms of application and declaration	94
Serving personnel—Instructions for claiming stars and medals	95

Civilian qualifying service in the United Kingdom—Defence Medal—
Preamble	96
Civil forms of application	97
Instructions for claiming the Defence Medal	98
Deceased personnel	99
Colonial Civil Defence Organizations	100

Appendices—
First Arakan Campaign—qualifying areas	A
North West Frontier of India—qualifying areas	B
Sea going vessels eligible for clasp North Africa, 1942-43	C
Civilian categories (United Kingdom) eligible for the Defence Medal	D

SECTION I

GENERAL

1. Preamble

This Pamphlet gives details of the conditions and qualifying areas for the award of campaign stars, clasps, emblems and medals instituted for the 1939-45 War, and is based on and amplifies for army requirements, the qualifying conditions laid down in White Paper Command 6833 and subsequent amendments thereto.

2. Classes Eligible for Awards

The following classes generally will be eligible to qualify for the above mentioned awards:—

(i) All officers and other ranks (including women's services) who served in the British or Commonwealth Military Forces.

(ii) Specified personnel of approved Colonial Military Forces, Militarized Police and Militarized Civilian Bodies.

(iii) V.A.D. officers and members employed by the Army Council for service in military medical establishments.

(iv) The specially approved members of civilian organizations and independent members as defined in para. 9 (i), who served with the forces in army operational commands overseas or with the forces overseas from or outside the territory of residence in a non-operational area subjected to enemy air attack or closely threatened. The approved categories of civilians referred to in para. 9 (iii) are eligible to qualify only for the Defence Medal.

(v) All officers and other ranks (including women's services) of the Indian Forces.

(vi) (*a*) Foreign nationals commissioned or enlisted as individuals into the British Forces.

(*b*) United States nationals in the American Field Service (*see* para. 9 (i) (*a*)).

3. Order of Wearing and Description of Ribbons and Emblems

(i) The order of precedence and a description of the ribbons of the stars, clasps and medals instituted for the 1939-45 War are as follows:—

The 1939-45 Star.—The ribbon of the 1939-45 Star is dark blue, red and light blue in three equal vertical stripes. The dark blue stripe is intended to mark the service of the Naval Forces and the Merchant Navy, the red stripe that of the Armies, and the light blue stripe that of the Air Forces. The ribbon is to be worn with the dark stripe furthest from the left shoulder.

The Atlantic Star.—The ribbon of the Atlantic Star is blue, white and sea green, shaded and watered, the design being intended as a symbol of service in the Atlantic. The ribbon is to be worn with the blue edge furthest from the left shoulder.

The Air Crew Europe Star.—The ribbon of the Air Crew Europe Star is light blue with black edges, and there is in addition a narrow yellow stripe on either side. The design is symbolic of the continuous service of the Air Forces by night and day.

The Africa Star.—The ribbon of the Africa Star is pale buff in colour, with a central vertical red stripe and two other narrower stripes, one dark blue and the other light blue. The background is intended as a symbol of the desert, the central red stripe stands for the Armies, the dark blue stripe for the Naval Forces and the Merchant Navy, and the light blue stripe for the Air Forces. The ribbon is to be worn with the dark blue stripe furthest from the left shoulder.

The Pacific Star.—The ribbon of the Pacific Star is dark green with red edges and with a central yellow stripe. There are also two other narrow stripes, one dark blue and the other light blue. The green and yellow stand for the forests and the beaches of the Pacific, the red edges for the Armies, the dark blue stripe for the Naval Forces and the Merchant Navies, and the light blue stripe for the Air Forces. The ribbon is to be worn with the dark blue stripe furthest from the left shoulder.

The Burma Star.—The ribbon of the Burma Star is dark blue with a central red stripe, and in addition two orange stripes. The red stands for the British Commonwealth Forces and the orange for the sun, and these are placed on a contrasting background of dark blue.

The Italy Star.—The ribbon of the Italy Star is in the Italian colours, green, white and red. There are five vertical stripes of equal width, one in red at either edge and one in green at the centre, the two intervening stripes being in white.

The France and Germany Star.—The ribbon of the France and Germany Star is in the red, white and blue of the Union Flag, and these colours are also used as a symbol of France and the Netherlands. There are five vertical stripes of equal width, one in blue at either edge and one in red at the centre, the two intervening stripes being in white.

The Defence Medal.—The ribbon of the Defence Medal is flame coloured in the centre, and the edges are green, symbols of the enemy attacks on our green and pleasant land. Two black stripes represent the black-out.

The War Medal 1939-45.—The ribbon of the War Medal 1939-45 is in the red, white and blue of the Union Flag. There is a narrow central red stripe with a narrow white stripe on either side. There are broad red stripes at either edge, the two intervening stripes being in blue.

The India Service Medal 1939-45.—The ribbon is in the blue colours of the Order of the Star of India and the Order of the Indian Empire. There is a narrow central light blue stripe with a narrow dark blue stripe on either side. There are broad dark blue stripes at either edge, the two intervening stripes being in light blue.

(ii) No individual may be awarded more than five of the eight campaign stars, as shown below:—

The 1939-45 Star.
The Africa Star.
The Pacific or Burma Star.
The Italy Star.
The France and Germany or Atlantic or Air Crew Europe Star.

(iii) The Defence Medal, the War Medal 1939-45, and the India Service Medal, 1939-45, if earned, may be granted in addition to campaign stars, but the India Service Medal 1939-45 may not be granted to anyone qualifying for the Defence Medal.

(iv) A description of the titles of the clasps awarded with campaign stars and of the emblems denoting them is as follows:—

Clasp	Emblem
Battle of Britain	Silver gilt rose.
Atlantic	Silver rose.
Air Crew Europe	Silver rose.
8th Army	8
1st Army	1
North Africa 1942-43	Silver rose.
Pacific	Silver rose.
Burma	Silver rose.
France and Germany	Silver rose.

Only one clasp may be awarded with each star. Only one emblem may be worn on the appropriate ribbon when the star is not worn.

4. Concurrent Service and Aggregation of Service

(i) Service qualifying for one star may not run concurrently with service qualifying for another star (except as in para. 10).

(ii) An individual, however, who has once completed the 180 days (60 days in the case of airborne personnel) operational service required for the award of the 1939-45 Star and has been awarded either the Atlantic Star or Air Crew Europe Star will not be required to complete a further period of qualifying service for the 1939-45 Star in order to begin qualifying for the other award. A similar arrangement applies to the prior service qualifications for awards of the Pacific, Burma and Italy Stars to personnel referred to in para. 7.

(iii) Service, which by reason of its special nature qualifies for a campaign star (para. 6 (ii) (*b*)), may not run concurrently with service qualifying for the Defence Medal (or in the case of Indian Army personnel, for the India Service Medal 1939-45).

(iv) Operational service on land, or at sea or in the air, may be aggregated towards the qualifying period required for the award of the 1939-45 Star.

Service on visits in excess of the 30 days required for a special award of a particular area campaign star may not be aggregated with service of under 30 days while on visits to other operational areas.

(v) Service in the various eligible categories may be aggregated for the award of the Defence Medal, provided that the periods of service were not concurrent.

Time spent in a non-operational area overseas from, or outside, the normal country of residence, amounting to less than that required for the particular area, may be aggregated, at its actual time value, with the qualifying service in the normal country of residence.

5. Land—Definitions of Qualifying Service

(i) *Definition of service which may qualify by entry into operational areas on land*

    (*a*) Service of personnel posted within a War Establishment of a unit or formation in an operational command within the qualifying period.

    (*b*) Service of personnel temporarily attached for duty to a unit or formation in an operational command within the qualifying period, the duty performed being of a similar nature to that of the unit or formation to which attached, and not being a visit of an advisory or inspectional nature, or a temporary break of journey whilst in transit.

(c) Service of personnel attached for duty in the operational area to carry out a specific duty required by the Commander-in-Chief. (Subject to para. (b) above.)

(d) During the period an individual is on the *posted strength* of a unit in the operational area, absence on temporary duty or war leave or casual leave or on a course of instruction in a non-operational area may be aggregated with other qualifying service towards the six months required for the 1939-45 Star.

(ii) *Visits, journeys and inspections*

(a) Visits, journeys and inspections will not be a qualification unless they amount to 30 days or more and were specially approved by the War Office, Admiralty, Air Ministry, or in a command comprising both operational and non-operational areas, by the Commander-in-Chief.

(b) In all cases where the visit on official military duty under orders lasted for 30 days or more, or in very special circumstances where the service *of less than 30 days was of unusual importance to, and in the fire zone of actual operations,* application may be made to the War Office (A.G. 4 Medals), for approval to reckon such service.

(c) Personnel employed on escort duty in prisoner of war ships will be eligible for the appropriate area campaign star if the total aggregate of days spent on shore in the military operational area amounted to 30 days or more.

(d) The 30 day rule mentioned in para. (ii) (b) above, does not qualify for the 1939-45 Star for service in France before the 10th May, 1940, or for service in any other operational areas where for this star a six months' qualifying period is required.

(e) Consideration will be given to applications for time spent on an approved visit to be aggregated with other *operational* service in order to complete the required time qualification of six or two months for the award of the 1939-45 Star.

(iii) *Journeys (land areas)*

(a) The service of an individual or a unit in transit through an army operational area will not be a qualification for the area campaign star unless at least 30 days were spent in the qualifying area. Application will be made to the War Office (A.G. 4 Medals) for approval in each case.

(b) Personnel sent from a non-operational to an army operational area for hospital treatment or for training at an O.C.T.U., or to a training unit (*e.g.,* from Palestine to Egypt), who were not subsequently posted for duty to a unit in the operational area during the qualifying period, may not reckon such service as a qualification for the area campaign star.

(iv) *Journeys to operational areas by sea*

(a) Journeys by army personnel (other than those specifically posted for sea-going duties) through sea areas of active operations to an army operational command, will count, from the date of embarkation, towards the qualifying period of six months required for the 1939-45 Star, provided the journey was completed and the date of arrival fell within the period that the area was operational.

(b) Those who did not complete the journey to the operational area owing to death, wounds, or injury due to *enemy action* will qualify for the 1939-45 Star under para. 10 but may not thereby be granted the campaign star appropriate to the area.

(v) *Journeys to non-operational areas by sea*

(a) Journeys by army personnel through operational and non-operational waters, to a non-operational land area may count as service qualifying for the Defence Medal, but such time may not count towards the qualifying period for the 1939-45 Star.

(b) For service on passage as in (v) (a) the same scale will be applied to voyages through operational and non-operational waters and will be counted at its full rate towards the qualifying period of three years for an award of the Defence Medal for service in the United Kingdom, or of a year for service overseas from, or outside, the country of residence, in a territory not classified as subjected to enemy attack or closely threatened.

(c) Service on passage as in (v) (a) to a non-operational territory overseas from, or outside, the country of residence, but classified as subjected to enemy attack or closely threatened, will, when the Defence Medal is claimed in respect of six months' service, be counted at half the actual time of the voyage.

(d) Personnel will be eligible for the special award of the Defence Medal under the conditions of para. 10 (ii) who, during service afloat in transit to a non-operational area, sustained as a result of enemy action a wound or injury qualifying for a wound stripe. Injuries sustained at sea which qualify for a wound stripe include the ill effects of immersion or exposure at sea in open boats which necessitated not less than a week of treatment in hospital.

(vi) For the purpose of assessing eligibility to campaign stars/medals:—

(a) " One month " or multiples thereof are deemed to be 30 days or multiples thereof, respectively.

(b) " Entry " into operational service on land is deemed to be the first day (or part thereof) of service in the qualifying area.

6. Air—Definitions of Qualifying Airborne Service

(i) Airborne troops of the Army, who have taken part in airborne operations, qualify for Campaign Stars under the following regulations. Service under these rules will qualify on posting within the establishment of, or attachment for duty to, a qualifying unit or formation as under:—

A.A.C.	Glider Pilot Regiment.
	Parachute Regiment.
	Special Air Service Regiment.

Airborne Corps or Divisional Troops.
(Any unit which was included in the Order of Battle of an Airborne or Parachute formation.)

Army Air Transportation Organization (Burma).

R.A.S.C.	Air Despatch Organization.
R.A.	Anti-Aircraft Air Liaison Staff at R.A.F. Headquarters.
	Pilots of Air Observation Posts who acted as flying artillery O.Ps.
Miscellaneous	Such other units as may be later defined.

(ii) (a) For airborne troops of the Army, a "sortie" is deemed to be a flight over enemy, or enemy occupied territory, or waters adjacent thereto and an "Airborne operation" means an operational sortie followed by a landing (i.e., entry into a qualifying land operational area) in which case, personnel qualify for the appropriate area campaign star by reason of such entry, and, in addition, for the 1939-45 Star, provided the completed period of two months (including the operational flight) has been spent in a fully operational unit (see para.(b)).

(b) For airborne troops an "operational unit" means a unit, in an operational or non-operational area (including the United Kingdom), which provided personnel for airborne operations. (A list of those airborne units and training units in non-operational areas that are deemed to be qualifying units will be promulgated.)

(c) Units in training, from which personnel, though ready for service, did not take part in operational sorties, are not regarded as operational units.

(iii) (a) In the Royal Air Force and for seconded or liaison service, an "operational unit" means a squadron, or a flight, but not a station or any superior headquarters.

(b) Personnel at an operational training unit (R.A.F.) who were required to make an operational sortie, may count their service at that unit from the date of the sortie onwards as qualifying service.

(c) Flights made only as passengers or observers will not qualify. It is essential that the flights be part of special operational tasks to be eligible for awards. The benefit of aircrew rules apply only to those with flying qualifications and who were posted to operational units for employment as members of air crew.

(d) For the award of the Air Crew Europe Star the expression "entry into operational service" is subject to the qualification that six or two months' operational service must already have been rendered (see para. 24).

(e) Under the terms of Air Ministry Order A. 471 of 1945 awards of the (then designated) 1939-43 Star or the Africa Star previously authorized to R.A.F. personnel are to be considered as cancelled. (Army personnel who were transferred from the Royal Air Force will be required to make a further claim on A.F. B 2070.)

(f) Applications for awards of campaign stars and the War Medal 1939-45 in respect of service as Civil Air Crew during the 1939-45 War should be made to the Ministry of Civil Aviation, S.P. Division (S.P. 1), Ariel House, Strand, W.C. 2.

7. Sea—Definitions of Qualifying Seagoing Service

(i) *Service afloat qualifying under Royal Navy Rules*

(a) *Permanent Ships' Staff*:—

Officers and other ranks of the Army appointed for specified sea-going duties, who served in H.M. ships, Royal Fleet auxiliaries, hired transports, hospital ships, hospital carriers, merchant fleet auxiliaries, tankers, defensively equipped merchant ships, or sea-going craft under army control, will qualify for campaign stars under rules appropriate to the Royal Navy. Service will begin to qualify from the date of embarkation for sea-going duties. Service under these rules will qualify on posting within the establishment of, or attachment for duty to, a qualifying unit or formation as under:—

Maritime R.A.
A.A. Defence of Merchant Shipping.
A.A.:L.M.G. Troops for the Defence of Ships in Government Service.

Permanent ships staff of Troopships or Hospital Ships or Carriers.
Bombardment Units R.A. attached to the Royal Navy.
Bombardment Units R.A. Combined operation. (Bombardment Liaison Officers.)

(b) *Special awards for service afloat*: —

Special awards of campaign stars for service afloat may be made under conditions appropriate to the Royal Navy, to army personnel as shown below.

Such service afloat is not a qualification for the Atlantic Star as it is not regarded as part of the Battle of the Atlantic.

1. Ferry paymasters R.A.P.C., who remained afloat, or, if they landed, did not perform duties in the qualifying operational area. (Ferry paymasters R.A.P.C., who accompanied operational troops to the operational commands and who performed their duties on land, are to be regarded as attached to the unit or formation for duty and to qualify for campaign stars under army rules.)
2. Military personnel serving in sea-going vessels operated by the Army or serving in motor boat companies R.A.S.C. (excluding military personnel undergoing training). (*See* para. 8 (ii)).
3. Military personnel who served in certain specified dredger companies R.E. (only the France and Germany Star) or in port repair ships in operational area ports overseas.
4. Personnel of tank ferry squadrons, or stores convoy detachments or anti-pilfering parties who, although held on the strength of a unit in a non-operational area, were employed *regularly* on sea-ferrying, etc., duties between non-operational and operational areas, provided they made more than one trip to the operational area in close support of the operations. Those who made only one trip will not be eligible for a special award, unless their duties required them to land in the operational area.
5. Miscellaneous duties, *e.g.*, draft conducting, performed by personnel whilst in transit as "passengers" will not qualify as service afloat for a campaign star.

(ii) *Definition of " entry into operational service " while serving afloat*

(a) For awards of the Atlantic, Pacific, Burma and Italy Stars for sea-going service, the expression "entry into operational service" is subject to the qualification that six months' operational service must already have been rendered. Certain modifications to these rules are mentioned in the text relating to particular stars.

(b) Sea-going service in vessels not operating in the areas qualifying for particular stars, but on the passage through those areas, or making occasional visits to the defined areas for fuelling and so forth, will be considered as "casual entry into the areas" and will not be regarded as qualifying service for the area campaign star. Time spent on such passage may be counted towards the period qualifying for the 1939-45 Star under para. 18.

(iii) *The general rules relating to army personnel serving afloat are as follows*: —

The expression "service afloat" means service while borne on the books of: —

(a) A ship of war in sea-going commission. (Service while refitting may count as "service afloat" provided that the ship remains in commission). Service in ships refitted in the United States of America may not count as "service afloat" but may count towards the Defence Medal. If the ship's company of a ship refitting in the United States is not reduced, any time served in the ship after the first three months of refitting shall count towards completion of qualification for the 1939-45 Star, or the Atlantic Star, if the star in question had begun to be earned before that date.

(b) A parent ship for service in commissioned tenders which are wholly or mainly employed on sea-going duties.

(c) A commissioned ship for such other sea-going service as may be declared to qualify for this purpose. In this category will be included:—

  (1) Service while embarked for duty in merchant ships (e.g., D.E.M.S. personnel, commodores of convoy and their staffs and permanent army ships staff of troopships and transports, etc.).

  (2) Service in *sea-going* boom defence and examination vessels.

  (3) Service afloat in combined operations craft as laid down in para. 8.

  (4) Service for liaison duties in allied sea-going ships of war.

  (5) Service in depot ships that have proceeded to ports *abroad* may be counted as "service afloat" for the purpose of qualifying for the 1939-45 Star only. Such service will be held to qualify for the Atlantic, Burma or Italy Star only if, in the opinion of the Admiralty, qualification is justified by circumstances as, for instance, ships of the British Pacific Fleet and Fleet Train which proceeded forward of Australia.

(d) Service afloat not qualifying for campaign stars

The following shall not be regarded as "service afloat" for the award of campaign stars but may be reckoned as qualifying service for the Defence Medal:—

  (1) Service in stationary depot ships which only went to sea proceeding from port to port (e.g., for the purpose of changing base for refit, etc.) except under para. 7 (iii) (c) (5) above.

  (2) Service at shore bases and depots.

  (3) Service in vessels employed wholly or mainly within boom protected waters, or where no boom existed, within the limits of smooth waters. Intermittent sea service in craft which proceeded only occasionally beyond shallow waters may not be aggregated with qualifying service for the 1939-45 Star.

  (4) Mine sweeping and patrol services in the Thames, or service with an A.A. Fort Regiment R.A. in estuaries throughout the United Kingdom.

  (5) Military personnel undergoing training at sea.

  (6) Military personnel posted for sea-going duties (*see* para. 7) who served in sea-going ships in non-operational sea areas and for periods during which they were thereby ineligible to qualify for campaign stars, may aggregate such service with service qualifying for the Defence Medal.

(e) Civilians

Civilian personnel serving in sea-going vessels operated by the Army will qualify for campaign stars under similar conditions to those required for Merchant Navy service, e.g.:—

(1) Service based in the United Kingdom, may not be reckoned as qualifying service for the Defence Medal.
(2) Intermittent service in craft which proceeded only occasionally beyond shallow waters may be aggregated towards qualifying service for the 1939-45 Star.

(f) British Merchant Seamen in Allied Ships

Service by a British seaman in an Allied ship, although not on charter to H.M. Government, may be accepted as qualifying service for the award of campaign stars and the War Medal 1939-45, provided that:—

(1) the seaman was engaged with the consent or approval of H.M. Government (e.g., the Merchant Navy Pool and British Consuls);
(2) the seaman produces satisfactory evidence of such service;
(3) the ship on which the service was performed was running in the Allied war effort;
(4) the seaman has not accepted, and will not be permitted to accept, equivalent Allied general awards in respect of any service during the war.

8. Combined Operations Personnel

(i) Officers and other ranks who took part afloat in combined operations but did not land will count service as for sea-going personnel under para. 7.

(ii) Time spent in sea-going vessels training for operations may be aggregated towards service qualifying for the Defence Medal.

(iii) Personnel of naval beach commandos and naval beach signal sections and other special combined operations units who served *ashore* qualify under Army rules.

(iv) Regular crews of combined operations craft, *viz.*, sea-going commissioned major landing craft crews, and personnel of sea-going minor landing craft flotillas and land barge flotillas, provided they have been to sea in their craft, qualify under Royal Navy rules.

9. Civilians

(i) *Specially approved civilian categories*

The specially approved civilian categories eligible for campaign stars and the War Medal 1939-45 for service in army operational commands, or for the Defence Medal and the War Medal 1939-45 for service overseas from or outside the territory of residence in a non-operational area subjected to enemy air attack or closely threatened, are as follows:—

(a) *Medical Services (Overseas)*

Joint War Organization of the British Red Cross Society and the Order of St. John of Jerusalem.
Chartered Physiotherapists (British Red Cross Society).
American Field Service (*see* para. 2).

(b) *Philanthropic Bodies* (*Overseas*)
   Army Scripture Readers' Association.
   Catholic Women's League.
   Christian Scientists (Officiating Ministers).
   Christian Scientists Welfare Workers (Librarians and Secretaries).
   Church Army.
   Church of England Soldiers', Sailors' and Airmen's Institute.
   Church of Scotland.
   Hibbert Houses.
   Incorporated Soldiers', Sailors' and Airmen's Help Society.
   Methodist and United Board Churches.
   Mission to Mediterranean Garrisons.
   Salvation Army.
   Soldiers', Sailors' and Airmen's Families Association.
   Toc H.
   Young Men's Christian Association.
   Young Women's Christian Association.

(c) *Voluntary Societies under the Council of the British Society for Relief abroad*
   Catholic Committee for Relief Abroad.
   Guide International Relief Service.
   International Voluntary Service for Peace.
   Jewish Committee for Relief Abroad.
   Joint War Organization of the British Red Cross Society and the Order of St. John of Jerusalem.
   Salvation Army.
   Save the Children Fund, Registered Charity.
   Scout International Relief Service.
   World Student Relief (also known as International Student Service) (London Committee).
   Young Women's Christian Association.

(d) *N.A.A.F.I.* (*Overseas*)
   N.A.A.F.I./Women's Voluntary Service.
   Civilian Uniformed Employees.
   Entertainment National Service Association (E.N.S.A.).

(e) *Other organizations and independent members* (*Overseas*)
   Allied Expeditionary Force Club.
   Army Schoolmistresses (Malta).
   Assistant Commissioners H.M. Forces War Savings Committee.
   Civil Defence Service/Overseas Column.
   Interpreters (*see* para. 9 (ii) (*c*)).
   National Fire Service/Overseas Column.
   Technical Representatives (Civilian) R.E.M.E.
   Telecom Personnel (Cable and Wireless Ltd.).
   War Correspondents (including Americans who served between 3.9.39 and 8.12.41 inclusive).
   War Office King's Messengers.
   Women's Voluntary Service/A.W.S.
   Women's Transport Service/A.W.S.
   Women's Transport Service/F.A.N.Y. (Special Parties).

(ii) *Conditions for awards.*

(a) It is a condition that civilians wore the approved civilian uniform of their organization, were full time workers, were subject in certain cases to military law and satisfied the conditions appropriate for military personnel. (Chartered Physiotherapists were permitted to wear the outdoor uniform of the B.R.C.S., or, if at the time of their acceptance for employment with the War Department they were members of the St. John's Ambulance Brigade or the St. Andrew's Ambulance Association, the uniform of that Brigade or Association instead of the uniform of the B.R.C.S.)

(b) A special exception is made for those entertainers sponsored by the D.N.S.E. or the War Office, who were sent overseas without uniform before July, 1943. They will be eligible for campaign stars provided they were eligible to wear the E.N.S.A. uniform after July, 1943, under the rules then adopted, or would have been so eligible had their service continued to that date. From July, 1943, the uniform requirement will be an essential qualification for all entertainers.

(c) Interpreters will be eligible if they wore military uniform, were paid from army funds and were employed full-time in a military organization, provided they are not eligible for a similar award from their own or any other Allied government.

Those employed with, or working alongside and closely associated with, civilian staff not eligible for campaign stars, will not themselves be eligible in respect of such service.

(d) Only members of W.T.S./F.A.N.Y. who were incorporated for special duties in overseas military establishments and W.T.S./A.W.S. who were employed on welfare duties in South East Asia Command will be eligible.

(e) Members of W.T.S./F.A.N.Y. who served as civilians in the Polish Forces under British Command will be eligible to qualify for British campaign stars. Those who served in non-operational areas overseas from the United Kingdom which were subjected to enemy air attack or closely threatened, will be eligible to qualify for the Defence Medal.

(iii) *United Kingdom Categories*

(a) The following classes of civilians who wore British Army uniform are eligible to qualify for the Defence Medal for *full-time* service in the United Kingdom.

Army Welfare Officers.
Assistant Record Officers.
Instructors of Senior or Junior Training Corps.
Lands Branch, War Office (commissioned personnel).
Officiating Chaplains (Civilian) appointed by the War Office (not in uniform).
Recruiting Officers and Army Recruiters (Army and A.T.S.).

(b) The following classes are eligible to qualify for the award of the Defence Medal for *part time* service in the United Kingdom:—

Home Guard (formerly Local Defence Volunteers).
L.A.A. Regiments—T.A. Reserve (when not embodied).
National Defence Companies (formerly National Defence Corps), T.A. Reserve, before embodiment or enlistment.
Isle of Man Home Guard.
Voluntary Interception Service/Radio Security Service.

(c) Home Guard service will count from the date of signing the Enrolment Form (A.F. W 3066). Members who joined the Local Defence Volunteers at its inception and performed duty before signing the form may count earlier service provided the member produces a certificate from an officer under whom he served in the Local Defence Volunteers at a date before that given on A.F. W 3066.

(d) Women Auxiliaries, Home Guard, may not count such service as qualifying for the Defence Medal.

(iv) *Colonial Police*

(a) Occupied Enemy Territory Administration Colonial Police and the former Palestine Police who performed service in operations in an operational command are eligible for campaign stars. (It is a condition that such service was approved by the military commander for the operational area during the qualifying period.)

(b) Personnel of the former Palestine Police Force are eligible to qualify for the War Medal 1939-45 for 28 days' service between 27th May, 1942, and 8th May, 1945, or the dates on which the force ceased to be militarized if earlier. (The former Palestinian Special Police are not included in this category.)

10. Special Awards

(i) *Campaign Stars*

(a) The normal qualifying conditions will be waived in the following circumstances and the awards granted will be the 1939-45 Star in addition to the campaign star appropriate to the area in which operational service was rendered by personnel,

  (1) who on account of such service have been awarded an honour, or decoration, or Mention in Despatches, or King's Commendation for brave conduct or King's Commendation for valuable service in the air, and the award has been published in the *London Gazette*, or

  (2) whose operational service was brought to an end by death, wounds or other disability due to service.

(b) The grant of an honour or decoration, etc., means a British "personal award" conferred by His Majesty the King. The award of a foreign decoration, etc., will not be a qualification for the award of campaign stars or medals.

(c) Army personnel granted King's Commendations for brave conduct for service in merchant ships (*i.e.*, A.A. Defence of Merchant Shipping and Maritime A.A.) which were published in the Civil Supplements of the *London Gazettes* before September, 1942, will qualify under para. 10 (i) (a) (1) above.

(d) The disability referred to in para. 10 (i) (a) (2) above must have been of sufficient gravity to cause evacuation beyond a regimental aid post, or in the case of base troops, admission to hospital, or in the case of sea going troops, discharge to shore.

(e) Wounded personnel who were captured and thereby prevented from being evacuated in the normal manner will be regarded as qualifying under para. 10 (i) (a) (2) above.

(f) All cases of evacuation as a result of self inflicted wounds or venereal disease will be forwarded to the War Office for decision.

(g) A special award of the 1939-45 Star under the conditions of paragraph 10 (i) (a) may not be granted to personnel referred to in the sub-para. 5 (ii) who were evacuated as a result of wounds or sickness incurred during the visit, journey or inspection.

(h) An individual granted an honour, decoration or Mention in Despatches, whose service generally was outside the operational zones, will not be granted a special award of campaign stars under the conditions of para. 10 (i) (a) (1) unless the time spent visiting an operational area amounted to a minimum of 30 days' duration (see. para. 5 (ii)).

(ii) *Defence Medal*

The normal qualifying conditions will be waived and a special award of the Defence Medal will be granted:—

(a) When service in an eligible category was brought to an end before the completion of the qualifying period either by death due to *enemy action* when on duty, or by injuries giving entitlement to a wound stripe as defined in A.C.I. 233 of 1944 (as amended).

(b) To those British subjects who have received a personal award as defined in para. 10 ((i) (a)) provided that the recipient, when the award or King's Commendation was *earned*, was serving in a category eligible for the Defence Medal and that the distinction was granted in respect of service qualifying for the Defence Medal.

(c) To recipients of the George Cross, or the George Medal, who were granted either of these awards for gallantry in Civil Defence, but who were not in a category which would qualify them for the Defence Medal. (This arrangement will not apply to holders of awards other than the George Cross or the George Medal, and will also not apply to those granted the George Cross or George Medal for actions in service qualifying for campaign stars.

(iii) *The War Medal* 1939-45

The normal qualifying conditions will be waived and a special award will be granted in the following circumstances:—

Armed Forces.

When 28 days' service have not been completed, but when a campaign star has been awarded.

Approved civilian categories.

(c) When service with the Forces in an army operational area or in a closely threatened non-operational area. (*cf.* para. 55), was terminated before the completion of 28 days, by death, sickness or wounds, *due to enemy action when on duty.*

(The award of a campaign star does not otherwise in itself give entitlement to the War Medal 1939-45, unless 28 days' approved service have been completed.)

(iv) *The India Service Medal* 1939-45

The normal qualifying conditions will be waived for personnel who were granted an honour, decoration, Mention in Despatches or King's Commendation, which has been published in the *London Gazette* or the *Gazette of India* or the *Burma Gazette*, provided the distinction was granted for service qualifying for the India Service Medal 1939-45.

11. Service in Enemy, or Enemy Occupied, or in Neutral Territories

(i) *Prisoners of War*

(a) Time spent as a prisoner of war in consequence of capture in operations may be counted towards the qualifying period for the 1939-45 Star, but such time will not be counted towards the period of six months' sea-going, or two months' air crew operational service, which must, in circumstances described in sub-paragraph (b) below, be completed before the grant of certain Stars may be authorized. Time spent as a prisoner of war may not qualify for the Defence Medal.

(b) Army personnel appointed for duty in seagoing vessels (*see* para. 7) or as air crew, who had completed the six or two months' operational service required for the award of the 1939-45 Star at the time of capture, may count time spent as a prisoner of war towards the period of six or two months' service required for the award of the Atlantic Star or the Air Crew Europe Star. That is to say, before capture they must have begun to earn one of these stars after completion of service required for the prior award of the 1939-45 Star.

(c) If service while a prisoner of war is certified by the War Office as "*similar to operational service against the enemy*", the appropriate area campaign star (but not the France and Germany Star for service before 6th June, 1944) may be awarded for such service.

(d) The grant of personal award as defined in para. 10 (i) (a) (1) for service in captivity, will not normally entitle the recipient to the special award of any campaign star. If, however, the service performed in captivity for which the award is granted, is deemed by the War Office to be of a nature similar to "*operational service against the enemy*" the recipient will be granted a special award of the appropriate area campaign star and the 1939-45 Star. The France and Germany Star may not, however, be granted for service of any kind before 6th June, 1944. Applications for awards under sub-paras. (i) (c) and (d) will be submitted to the War Office A.G. 4 (Medals), for decision.

(ii) *Personnel who escaped or were liberated from captivity, or who evaded capture*

(a) Personnel, after escape, evasion or liberation from captivity, may count such time towards the qualifying period for the 1939-45 Star. They will not otherwise be eligible for a further campaign star for such time, unless it is shown that during the period they took an active part in a fighting partisan organization, or in officially organized operations under arms in a forward zone during, or after, the process of escape or liberation.

(b) Time spent interned in neutral territory is not reckoned as time spent as a prisoner of war. Time spent, however, escaping or evading capture in a neutral country will not be reckoned, except after escape from enemy territory.

(c) Consideration will be given to applications for a special award of the appropriate area campaign star when the detailed report by the senior British officer, who was actually in charge of, and present with, the party when the operational service was performed shows that the individual took an active part in operations against the enemy When a British officer was not present during service with a fighting partisan organization, documentary evidence by a *responsible* witness who has first-hand knowledge of the service claimed will be submitted. Operational service by liberated ex-prisoners of war will be treated in the same way as service rendered by escapers or evaders. Every case for consideration will be the subject of examination.

(d) The grant of a personal award (as defined in para. 10 (i) (a) (1)) for escaping *and subsequent operational service* (but not for escaping only) will qualify the recipient for the 1939-45 Star and subject to the conditions laid down in paras. (i) (c) and (d) above for the appropriate area star.

(e) Campaign stars will not be awarded under the above rules to persons who were not in a category eligible for campaign stars before internment or entry into enemy occupied territory.

(f) All claims for service as above will be submitted to the War Office A.G. 4 (Medals) for consideration.

(iii) *Special Operations Executive Personnel and those engaged in clandestine operations*

Application for campaign stars for special service in enemy or enemy occupied territories by personnel other than those specified above will be submitted to the War Office A.G. 4 (Medals) for consideration.

12. Allied and Other Foreign Nationals

(i) *The Campaign Stars and the War Medal 1939-45*

(a) The categories of Allied and other foreign nationals eligible for British campaign stars and the War Medal 1939-45 are stated at para. 2.

(b) Awards are made on the understanding that individuals do not receive a similar award from their own or any other Allied government. A similar award is to be interpreted as a campaign star or commemorative medal instituted for the period and for the service for which a British star or medal has been instituted. The continued wearing of the ribbon of the British award will be invalidated by the acceptance of any other award as above defined.

(c) Foreign nationals who subsequently transferred to the forces of their own countries must, in order to qualify, have completed their qualifying service before their own countries declared war. Citizens of the United States of America who served in the British Armed Forces before 8th December, 1941, and who before transfer to the United States Armed Forces, qualified for British campaign stars and medals, may be granted the appropriate awards in addition to any awards that may have been subsequently granted to them by the United States Government. In these cases para. (b) above will not apply.

(d) Polish Officers and other ranks who served under British command, whether they have volunteered to return to Poland, or have become members of the Resettlement Corps in the United Kingdom, are eligible to qualify for British campaign stars and medals.

(ii) *The Defence Medal*

(a) Foreign nationals who served in the British Forces (para. 2) will be eligible for the Defence Medal, subject to sub-para. (c) below, on the same terms as British Army personnel.

(b) Foreign civilian subjects who were required to carry out, or who voluntarily undertook, civil duties for which the Defence Medal is awarded will be eligible, regardless of nationality, and they will be awarded the medal, subject to sub-para. (c) below, on the same terms as British civilians.

(c) In the case of Foreign nationals who sought refuge in the United Kingdom during the 1939-45 War, for instance in 1940, the country of *refuge* will be regarded as the country of *residence* and the whole three years must have been served therein to qualify for the medal.

(d) The special qualifying conditions for Polish Forces under British command are given in para. 60.

13. Disqualification and Forfeiture

(i) The conditions for the forfeiture and restoration of campaign stars, the Defence Medal or the War Medal 1939-45 in respect of army personnel are as laid down in A.C.I. **1003** of 1947.

(ii) *The Defence Medal*

(a) Home Guard.—Members of the Home Guard who were dismissed or discharged on account of misconduct, or who left Home Guard service in contravention of an order made under Defence Regulations, or who failed persistently to perform duty which they were under obligation to perform, shall be liable to be disqualified for the Defence Medal to which they might otherwise be entitled.

(b) Civilians.—Civilians are liable to forfeit the Defence Medal on a conviction for treason or treachery (including offences under the Treachery Act of 1940, or for voluntarily aiding the enemy, or for serious offences under the Official Secrets Act).

SECTION II

1939-45 STAR

14. General

The 1939-45 Star is granted to recognize services rendered in operations during the War from the 3rd September, 1939, to the 2nd September, 1945, inclusive. The qualification is 180 days' operational service, except that a special award is granted for entry into operational service in certain specified areas and operations, or under the conditions laid down in para. 10.

Qualifying Land Areas (180 days)

(i) The qualification for army personnel for service *on land* is 180 days as part of the establishment in an army operational command in:—

(a) France between 3rd September, 1939, and 9th May, 1940, inclusive; or,

(b) any land operational area qualifying for the Africa, Pacific, Burma, Italy or France and Germany Star between the 3rd September, 1939, and 2nd September, 1945 (inclusive);

(c) qualifying service between 9th May, 1945, and 2nd September, 1945 (inclusive) may be aggregated with qualifying service prior to these dates.

Notes.—(a) The following areas in the Eastern Hemisphere will not be regarded as having been in the area of operational commands:—
Australia, Ceylon, Fanning Island, Fiji Islands, India (except the

North-West Frontier region and parts of Assam and Bengal), New Caledonia, New Hebrides, New Zealand, Norfolk Island, Phœnix Islands, Tonga Island.

(b) The rules for counting time spent in transit or as a prisoner of war and the conditions for " special awards " are stated in Section I.

(ii) Full time paid members of the specially approved colonial military forces, militarized police or militarized civilian bodies eligible to qualify for area campaign stars under sub-paras. 26 (ii) and (iii), 31 (ii) and 37 (ii), will also be eligible to qualify for the 1939-45 Star by 180 days under para. 14 (i) or one day under para. 15 for operational service during the qualifying period laid down for the force concerned.

(iii) The undermentioned force(s) are eligible to qualify for the 1939-45 Star under para. 15 for full time service during the periods shown:—

Arab Legion (Transjordan) ... ... 10.4.41-31.5.41.
8.6.41.-11.7.41.

(Provided a similar award is not granted for service in Iraq or Syria).

5. Qualifying Special Areas (one day)

In the following operations entry into operational service (*i.e.*, one day or part thereof) qualifies for the special award of the 1939-45 Star.

(i) *Europe*

		From	To
Ambleteuse	(Pas de Calais)	27. 7.41	28. 7.41
Anse de St. Martin	(Manche)	1. 3.43	2. 3.43
Belgium		10. 5.40	19. 6.40
Biville	(Seine Inferieure)	26.11.43	27.11.43
		26.12.43	27.12.43
Boulogne Berek	(Pas de Calais)	24. 6.40	25. 6.40
Boulogne-Le Touquet		3. 6.42	
Bordeaux	(Gironde)	7.12.43	
Bray Dunes	(Belgium)	16. 5.44	17. 5.44
Bruneval		27. 2.42	28. 2.42
Burhou	(Channel Islands)	7. 9.42	
Casquets Lighthouse	(C.I.)	2. 9.42	3. 9.42
Clomfjord (Lat. 66° 48′ N. Long 14° 01′ E.)	(Norway)	20. 9.42	21. 9.42
Dieppe		19. 8.42	
Dirrible Bay	(Sark)	25.12.43	26.12.43
Eletot (near)	(Seine Inferieure)	3. 8.43	6. 8.43
		1. 9.43	4. 9.43
France		10. 5.40	19. 6.40
Greece and Crete		*10. 3.41	31. 5.41
Guernsey	(C.I.)	14. 7.40	15. 7.40
Hardelot		21. 4.42	22. 4.42
Hardelot-Morilmont	(Pas de Calais)	30. 8.41	31. 8.41
Herm	(C.I.)	27. 2.43	28. 2.43
Holland		12. 5.40	13. 5.40
Houlgate Area	(Calvados)	23.11.41	24.11.41
Les Hemmes	(Pas de Calais)	16. 5.44	17. 5.44
Lillebo Stord (Lat. 59° 51′ N. Long. 5° 19′ E.)	(Norway)	23. 1.43	

* 7.11.40 for Air Transport and Ferrying Service.

		From	To
Lofoten Islands		4. 3.41 26.12.41	
Lucania	(Italy)	10. 2.41	
Morlaix Aerodrome	(Finisterre)	16.10.42	
Norway		14. 4.40	8. 6.40
Onival	(Somme)	3. 7.43 26.12.43 17. 5.44	27.12.43 18. 5.44
Petit Port	(Jersey)	25.12.43	26.12.43
Pointe de Gravelines	(Nord)	24.12.43	25.12.43
Pointe de Plouzec	(Cote de Nord)	11.11.42	12.11.42
Pointe de Saire (N.W. of)	(Manche)	14. 8.42	15. 8.42
Port-en-Bessin (W. of)	(Calvados)	12. 9.42	13. 9.42
Port St. Quentin (Quend Plage).	(Somme)	27.12.43	29.12.43
Quend Plage	(Somme)	15. 5.44	16. 5.44
Quineville	(Manche)	26.12.43	27.12.43
Sark		3.10.42	4.10.42
Sicily		10. 7.43	17. 8.43
Spitzbergen		25. 8.41 16. 5.42	3. 9.41 8. 9.43
St. Aubin	(Seine Inferieure)	27. 8.41	28. 8.41
St. Laurent	(Calvados)	11. 1.42	
St. Laurent-Vierville	(Calvados)	17. 1.44	21. 1.44
St. Nazaire		27. 3.42	28. 3.42
St. Vaast	(Seine Inferieure)	27. 8.41	28. 8.41
St. Valery En Caux (West of).	(Seine Inferieure)	2. 9.43	3. 9.43
Ushant (I d'Oussant)	(Finisterre)	3. 9.43	4. 9.43
Vaagso		27.12.41	
Vemork (90 miles W. of Oslo)	(Norway)	19.11.42	
Wassenaer	(S. Holland)	27. 2.44	28. 2.44

(ii) *Middle East*

	From	To
Iraq	10. 4.41	31. 5.41
Madagascar (with Comoro Islands)	5. 5.42	5.11.42
Persia	25. 8.41	28. 8.41
Syria	8. 6.41	11. 7.41

(iii) *India and Burma*

	From	To
Burma (Enemy Invasion)	22. 2.42	15. 5.42
Burma (First Arakan Campaign) (*see* Appendix A).	1.12.42	31. 5.43
Burma (Brig. Wingate's Force)	7. 2.43	15. 7.43
Burma (Special Force, Generals Wingate and Lentaigne).	15. 2.44	27. 8.44
India (North West Frontier) (*see* Appendix B)	3. 2.40 18. 6.41 28. 7.42	24. 5.40 26. 8.41 18. 8.42
Malaya (Enemy Invasion)	8.12.41	15. 2.42

(iv) *Pacific Theatre (Oceania)*   From   To

	From	To
Aleutian Islands (Air Crew only)	3. 6.42	16. 8.43
Bismarck Archipelago (Enemy Invasion)	22. 1.42	24. 1.42
Bismark Archipelago (Allied Invasions)—		
Admiralty Islands	29. 2.44	18. 5.44
Emirau Island	20. 3.44	20. 3.44
Mussau Island	30. 3.44	8. 4.44
British North Borneo Brunei Sarawak and Dutch Borneo (Enemy Invasion)	*8.12.41	3. 4.42
Caroline Islands (Allied Invasions)—		
Angaur	17. 9.44	20. 9.44
Ngulu	16.10.44	16.10.44
Palau	6. 9.44	14.10.44
Peleliu	15. 9.44	30. 9.44
Ulithi	21. 9.44	21. 9.44
Celebes (Enemy Invasion)	26. 1.42	26. 2.42
Gilbert Islands—		
Abaiang (Enemy Invasion)	10.12.41	24.12.41
Abomana (Allied Invasion)	21.11.43	25.11.43
Butaritari (Enemy Invasion)	10.12.41	12.12.41
Makin (Allied Invasion)	21.11.43	25.11.43
Tarawa		
(Enemy Invasion)	10.12.41	27. 9.42
(Allied Invasion)	21.11.43	25.11.43
Hong Kong (Enemy Invasion)	8.12.41	25.12.41
Iwo Jima (Allied Invasion)	19. 2.45	16. 3.45
Java (Enemy Invasion)	†5. 3.42	9. 3.42
Marianas Islands (Allied Invasions)—		
Guam	21. 7.44	10. 8.44
Saipan	15. 6.44	18. 7.44
Tinian	24. 7.44	1. 8.44
Molucca Islands (Enemy Invasion)	30. 1.42	26. 2.42
Morotai (Allied Invasion)	15. 9.44	5.12.44
Nauru (Enemy Invasion)	8.12.41	1. 3.42
Ocean Island (Enemy Invasion)	8.12.41	26. 8.42
Okinawa (Allied Invasion)	1. 4.45	21. 6.45
Philippine Islands (including outer islands) (Allied Invasion).	20.10.44	4. 7.45
Solomon Islands (British Solomon Islands Protectorate) (and Australian Mandated Territories)—		
Buka (Enemy Invasion)	1. 2.42	30. 4.42
Bougainville (Enemy Invasion)	1. 2.42	30. 4.42
Choiseul (Enemy Invasion)	1. 2.42	31. 5.42
Choiseul (Allied Raid)	28.10.43	4.11.43
Florida (with Tulagi Harbour) (Enemy Invasion).	1. 2.42	31. 5.42
Florida (with Tulagi Harbour) (Allied Invasion).	1. 8.42	31. 8.42
Green Islands (Allied Invasion)	15. 2.44	19. 2.44
Guadalcanal (Enemy Invasion)	1. 2.42	31. 5.42
Guadalcanal (Allied Invasion)	7. 8.42	9. 2.43

---

* 17.12.41 for Air Transport and Ferrying Service.
† 27.2.42 for Australian Military Forces.

	From	To
Malaita (Enemy Invasion)	1. 2.42	31. 5.42
New Georgia (Enemy Invasion)	1. 2.42	31. 5.42
New Georgia (Allied Invasion)	28. 6.43	13.10.43
Shortland (Enemy Invasion)	1. 2.42	30. 4.42
Treasury Group (with Mono) (Enemy Invasion).	1. 2.42	31. 5.42
Treasury Group (with Mono) (Allied Invasion)	25.10.43	26.11.43
Vangunu (Enemy Invasion)	1. 2.42	31. 5.42
Vangunu (Allied Invasion)	28. 6.43	13.10.43
Vella Lavella (Enemy Invasion)	1. 2.42	31. 5.42
Vella Lavella (Allied Invasion)	28. 6.43	13.10.43
Sumatra (Enemy Invasion)	14. 2.42	23. 3.42
Timor (Enemy Invasion)	20. 2.42	31. 3.42

16. Airborne Service

(i) Airborne troops will qualify for the 1939-45 Star if they have taken part in an airborne operation against the enemy, subject to the completion of 60 days' service in a fully operational unit. It is immaterial whether the operational unit was stationed in the United Kingdom, in an operational area or non-operational area. Personnel of airborne divisions who do not qualify for the 1939-45 Star (under para. 6 (ii)), and who joined up with the airborne portion of the division in action on the ground will be subject to the normal qualifying conditions of the Army. Personnel who took part in an airborne operation prior to completing the required period of two months' service with a fully operational unit and who were withdrawn from the operational area prior to qualifying for the 1939-45 Star, under normal army conditions, may aggregate any further service with a fully operational unit in order to complete the two months required for this award.

In cases where prior to joining an air operational unit, operational service of over four months has been rendered elsewhere, service in the air operational unit may be added to this former service in order to qualify for the 1939-45 Star under the 180 day rule.

(ii) (a) Personnel, who although airborne did not land in the operational area and, therefore, did not carry out an "airborne operation" as defined in sub-para. 6 (ii) will be required to make a second operational sortie during the two months' service with a fully operational unit to qualify for the 1939-45 Star.

Personnel at an air operational *training unit* (para. 6 (ii) (b)) will count service from the date of the sortie onwards.

(b) Units which were training, though ready for service will not necessarily be regarded as operational units. Service on return to a training, or a reserve unit will not qualify.

(iii) Liaison (etc.) officers at operational headquarters who flew regularly on operations and completed 60 days' service must have taken part as members of aircrew, but not as passengers or observers, in at least *three* operational sorties within the period of six consecutive months.

(iv) (a) The qualification for flying personnel posted or employed on air transport or ferrying duties will be 180 days' flying on approved overseas transport or approved ferrying routes (including at least three such overseas flights) during the period from 3rd September, 1939, to 2nd September, 1945, or a shorter period under the conditions of para. 10.

(b) For this purpose Trans-Atlantic flights; flights of a nature which would qualify for the Africa, Pacific, Burma, Italy or France and Germany Stars; flights to Norway, Sweden or Russia, or across the Bay of Biscay to Spain,

Portugal and beyond, and including flights on the Foynes-Bathurst route; or flights on the Darwin-Calcutta portion of the Empire Air Service Route during the period 8th December, 1941, to 2nd September, 1945; will be deemed to have been flights on approved routes. Flights from the United Kingdom to Eire will *not* be regarded as overseas flights for this purpose. For the period from 9th May, 1942, to 2nd September, 1945 (inclusive), qualifying service will be confined to flights involving landings in the prescribed operational land areas for the Pacific and Burma Star.

(c) The 1939-45 Star may also be awarded to those who took part in any of the special operations listed in para. 15 and made three or more landings in any prescribed area within the dates indicated. Participation in the evacuation of the Channel Islands between 19th and 21st June, 1940, will qualify subject to the completion of three landings on the islands during this period. Aggregations of landings in various operations is *not* permissible.

Note.—The rules for counting time spent as a prisoner of war, or evading capture, or after escape, or liberation and the conditions for the special award of this Star are stated in Section I.

17. Clasp to the 1939-45 Star

(i) The clasp to the 1939-45 Star is granted only for personnel who flew in fighter aircraft engaged in the Battle of Britain between 10th July and 31st October, 1940.

Personnel who flew in aircraft other than fighters, notwithstanding that they may have been engaged with the enemy in the air during the qualifying period, are not eligible for this clasp.

(ii) The award of the clasp and the silver gilt rose emblem denoting the clasp, are confined to those who operated with the undermentioned squadrons: —

Nos. 1, 17, 19, 23, 25, 29, 32, 41, 43, 46, 54, 56, 64, 65, 66, 72, 73, 74, 79, 85, 87, 92, 111, 141, 145, 151, 152, 213, 219, 222, 229, 234, 235, 236, 238, 242, 248, 249, 253, 257, 264, 266, 302, 303, 310, 312, 401 (No. 1 R.C.A.F. Sqn.), 501, 504, 600, 601, 602, 603, 604, 605, 607, 609, 610, 611, 615, 616, and the Fighter Interception Unit.

Awards will be made only with the approval of the Air Ministry.

18. Sea-going Service

The qualification for army personnel posted for duty in sea-going vessels (para. 7) is 180 days' service afloat in areas of active operations (dangerous waters).

19. Qualifying Sea Areas

(i) The qualifying sea areas for the 1939-45 Star are: —

(a) From the 3rd September, 1939, to the 31st May, 1940, the Atlantic Ocean, including Home Waters and the North Sea; the Baltic; the Arctic Ocean between Greenland and Longitude 70° E. and that part of the Indian Ocean lying South of 15° S. and West of 55° E.

(b) From the 1st June, 1940, to the 9th June, 1940, as (i) (a), with the addition of the Pacific Ocean and the rest of the Indian Ocean.

(c) From the 10th June, 1940, to the 8th May, 1945, anywhere at sea.

(d) From the 9th May, 1945, to the 2nd September, 1945, the areas are the Pacific Ocean, including the South China Sea, and the Indian Ocean and the Bay of Bengal, East of a line running from the southern-most point of Ceylon for a distance of 300 miles South, thence to a point 300 miles West of the southern-most point of Sumatra, and continuing East to the western side of Sunda Strait, thence through Christmas Island, and southwards along the Meridian of 110° E. (most of the Indian Ocean is excluded).

(ii) (a) Operational service on land may be aggregated with sea-going service. Service *afloat* in the operations listed in para. 15 may be aggregated towards the 180 days' qualifying period.

(b) Time spent as a " passenger " to a non-operational area is not qualifying service.

Note.—The rules for counting time spent in transit, or as a prisoner of war, or in evading capture, or after escape or liberation and the conditions for special awards are stated in Section I.

THE ATLANTIC STAR

20. General

The Atlantic Star is intended to commemorate the Battle of the Atlantic during the period 3rd September, 1939, to 8th May, 1945, and is designed primarily for convoys and their escorts and anti-submarine forces, as well as for fast merchant ships that sailed alone.

Sea-going Service

(i) The qualification for army personnel posted for duty in sea-going vessels (para. 7) is 12 months' (360 days') operational service, any six months of which were in the areas defined in para. 21. The Atlantic Star may not be awarded unless the 1939-45 Star has been qualified for by 180 days' operational service on land or afloat in addition to the 180 days' afloat required for the Atlantic Star, except for special awards under para. 10.

(ii) Those who were awarded the 1939-45 Star for less than six months' service in the land operations listed at para. 15, or for a special award under para. 10 (other than in the Atlantic Star areas), must complete the remaining portion of six months in order to aggregate a total of 360 days.

(iii) *Last six months:*—

Personnel (as defined in para. 7) who entered operational service in the qualifying area between 10th November, 1944, and 8th May, 1945, and did not subsequently serve in any other area of active operations may (subject to the rule as to casual entry at para. 7 (ii) (b)), qualify for the Atlantic Star by " entry into the area " and the six months' time qualification is waived. In such cases, except for a special award under para. 10 (i), the 1939-45 Star may not be awarded for service of less than six months.

21. Qualifying Areas

(i) The qualifying areas for the Atlantic Star are:—.

  (a) The Atlantic and Home Waters (*excluding any time served in the Mediterranean*).
  (b) The South Atlantic between longitude of Cape Horn (South America) and longitude 20° East (South Africa).
  (c) The convoy routes to ports in North Russia.

(ii) Service which, in the opinion of the Admiralty was not service in the Battle of the Atlantic, will *not* be a qualification, *e.g.*:—

  (a) Service in sea-going boom defence and in examination vessels employed solely for the defence of a port (such service is recognized by the 1939-45 Star).

(b) Service in vessels which were employed in, or in the vicinity of estuarial waters, or in particular localities, such as pilot cutters, light vessels, tugs engaged in port work and barges working in and around the mouth of the Thames.
(c) Service in Force H, after 9th November, 1942.
(d) Service afloat on or after 6th June, 1944, South of a line from the Firth of Forth to Kristiansand (South), in the English Channel or in the Bay of Biscay, East of longitude 6° West (since it qualifies for the alternative award of the France and Germany Star or Clasp).

22. Airborne Service

(i) The qualification for army personnel who were posted for aircrew duties (para. 6) is four months' (120 days') service in an air operational unit, 60 days of which was service in an air operational unit engaged in operations against the enemy over the areas defined in para. 21 (i) above. At least one qualifying sortie must have been made during the period of the 60 days. The Atlantic Star may not be awarded unless the 1939-45 Star has been qualified for by either (a) 60 days' service in an air operational unit in addition to the 60 days required for the Atlantic Star, or (b) 180 days' operational service elsewhere in addition to the 60 days' air operational service required for the Atlantic Star.

(ii) Where (notwithstanding the grant of the special award under paras. 10 and 15) operational service of over four months (but under 180 days) has been rendered elsewhere, before joining an air operational unit, service in the air operational unit may be added to this former service in order to qualify for the 1939-45 Star under the 180 days' rule, and service may then be aggregated to qualify for the Atlantic Star. *Note.*—Although air service may be added to army service to qualify for the 1939-45 Star under the 180 days' rule, army service may not be added to air service to qualify for this award under the 60 days' rule.

(iii) Last two months.—Air Crew unable to complete the 60 days required for the Atlantic Star under para. 22 (i) above, who entered operational service at any time between the 9th March, 1945 and 8th May, 1945, inclusive, and did not subsequently serve in any other operational area, will qualify for the Atlantic Star if they flew in operations against the enemy and the two months' time qualification will be waived. In such cases, except for a special award under para. 10, the 1939-45 Star may not be awarded for service of less than two months.

Note.—The rules for counting time spent as a prisoner of war, or evading capture, or after escape or liberation, and the conditions for the special award of this star are stated in Section I.

23. Clasps (Alternative Awards)

(i) Personnel qualifying for the Atlantic Star, the Air Crew Europe Star or the France and Germany Star, or two of these stars, will be awarded only the campaign star for which they *first* qualified. They will, however, be awarded a clasp to show that they rendered qualifying service for a second star. A further clasp will not be awarded to those who rendered service which would have qualified for the third star.

(ii) A silver rose emblem denoting the clasp will be worn on the ribbon of the campaign star awarded, when the star itself is not worn.

(iii) Personnel who made air sorties against targets on land and at sea from the same unit, do not thereby qualify for both the Atlantic Star and the Air Crew Europe Star. In such cases, the star appropriate to the normal function of the unit at the material time will be awarded *without* a clasp, except where the latter has been earned by other service. Cases of difficulty in applying this rule will be referred to the War Office (A.G. 4 (Medals)), for decision before an award is made.

THE AIR CREW EUROPE STAR

24. General

The Air Crew Europe Star is granted for operational flying from United Kingdom bases over Europe (including the United Kingdom) from the 3rd September, 1939, to the 5th June, 1944 (inclusive).

Airborne Service

(i) The qualification for army personnel who were posted for aircrew duties (para. 6) is four months' (120 days') service (except as in para. (ii) below) in a R.A.F. operational unit, 60 days of which was service in an operational unit engaged in operational flying over the area defined above. At least one qualifying sortie must have been made during the period of 60 days. The Air Crew Europe Star may not be awarded until the 1939-45 Star has been qualified for by either (*a*) 60 days' service in an air operational unit in addition to the 60 days required for the Air Crew Europe Star, or (*b*) not less than 180 days' operational service elsewhere, in addition to the 60 days' service required for the Air Crew Europe Star (notwithstanding the grant of a special award under para. 10 (i) or 15).

(ii) In cases where before joining an air operational unit, operational service of over four months (but under 180 days) has been rendered *elsewhere*, service in the air operational unit may be added to this former service in order to qualify for the 1939-45 Star under the 180 days' rule, and service may then be aggregated to qualify for the Air Crew Europe Star.

Notes.

(*a*) Although air service may be added to army service to qualify for the 1939-45 Star under the 180 days' rule, army service may not be added to air service to qualify for this award under the 60 days' rule.

(*b*) The rules for counting time spent as a prisoner of war or evading capture, or after escape or liberation and the conditions of the special award of this star are stated in Section I.

25. Clasps (Alternative Awards)

(i) Personnel qualifying for the Air Crew Europe, the France and Germany or the Atlantic Star, or two of these stars, will be awarded only the campaign star for which they *first* qualified. They will, however, be awarded a clasp to show that they rendered qualifying service for a second star. A further clasp will not be awarded to those who rendered service which would have qualified for the third star.

(ii) A silver rose emblem, denoting the award of the clasp, will be worn on the riband of the Campaign Star awarded, when the star itself is not worn.

(iii) Personnel who made sorties against targets on land and at sea from the same unit do not thereby qualify for both the Air Crew Europe Star and the Atlantic Star. In such cases the star appropriate to the normal function of the unit at the material time will be awarded *without* a clasp, except when the latter has been earned by other service. Cases of difficulty in applying this rule will be referred to the War Office (A.G. 4 Medals) for decision before an award is made.

THE AFRICA STAR

26. General

The Africa Star is granted for operational service in North Africa during the period from 10th June, 1940, to the 12th May, 1943, inclusive. The whole of the area between the Suez Canal and the Straits of Gibraltar is included, together with Malta, Abyssinia, The Somalilands and Eritrea.

Land Service

(i) The qualification for army personnel is entry as part of the establishment into operational service in areas defined in para. 27.

(ii) The undermentioned categories are also eligible to qualify for the Africa Star by virtue of entry into operational service (*i.e.*, a one-day qualification), between 10th June, 1940, and 27th November, 1941:—

Sudan Defence Force.
  (Members of the full-time permanent Force, who served anywhere in the Sudan.)

Combatant irregular Forces:—
  Banda Bukr or Bukr Force (Gedaref and Galabat area),
  Banda Fung (Kurmuk area),
  Frostyforce (Kassala Province Frontier area),
  Meadowforce (the hills west of the littoral in the Port Sudan and Tokar districts),
  Upper Nile Scouts (Upper Nile Frontier area),
  (provided members of these Forces served continuously on a full-time basis).

Sudan Auxiliary Defence Force.
  (Officers and warrant officers who commanded Sudan Police and other military personnel in active operations against the enemy, whether or not they were actually paid from army funds.)
  (Part-time service in, for instance, an anti-aircraft unit does not so qualify. The service must have been service in command of a unit earning campaign stars.)

(iii) The undermentioned categories are eligible to qualify for the Africa Star for 30 days' full-time operational service in the Sudan in areas shown in para. 27 (ii) (*a*), (*b*) or (*c*) during the period 10th June, 1940, to 27th November, 1941:—

Sudan Police, including Provincial and Railway Police (personnel embodied as part of the Sudan Defence Force).
Volunteers enrolled in the Sudan Auxiliary Defence Force (provided the volunteer personally served continuously on a full-time basis. The S.A.D.F. full-time paid units were the medical corps, the M.T. signals, interpreters and marine units).

27. Qualifying Land Areas

The qualifying areas for the Africa Star are:—

	From	To
(i) North Africa (troops under Allied Force Headquarters, and Middle East Command excluding formations not West of the Suez Canal and Red Sea).	10.6.40	12. 5.43
Malta	10.6.40	12. 5.43
Abyssinia (including attacks on Moyale, Elwak and Kassala).	10.6.40	27.11.41
Anglo-Egyptian Sudan (*see* para. 26 (i), (ii))	10.6.40	27.11.41
Eritrea	10.6.40	27.11.41
The Somalilands	10.6.40	27.11.41
Kenya (excluding Tanganyika territory and Uganda, except to troops who the G.O.C.-in-C., East Africa is satisfied were called forward from Uganda for operations in Lake Rudolf Area).	10.6.40	27.11.41
(ii) Sudan (*see* para. 26 (iii))	10.6.40	27.11.41

(a) Kassala Province South of a line drawn to the South of Suakin, Erkowit and Summit, and thence along the railway line to the Provincial boundary East of Atbara.

(b) Blue Nile Province East of the White Nile, and South of a line drawn from just South of Jebelein Eastwards to Abu Na'ama and then North-East to the River Ramad; or

(c) Upper Nile and Equatorial Provinces East of the Nile (excluding Nimule).

Notes.
(a) Service in West Africa is *not* a qualification.
(b) The conditions for a special award of the Africa Star for 30 days in the qualifying areas for visits, journeys and inspections are stated in Section I.

28. Airborne Service

(i) (a) The qualification for airborne troops is entry into operational service in the qualifying area.

(b) Army personnel who served as air crew will qualify by a sortie over North Africa or the Mediterranean.

(ii) The qualification for flying personnel posted or employed on air transport or ferrying duties during the qualifying period 10th June, 1940 to 12th May, 1943 (inclusive) will be:—

   (a) three flights over enemy occupied territory in Africa; or
   (b) three flights over operational land areas in Africa; or
   (c) three flights between Malta and Gibraltar, or between Malta and Egypt including three landings in Malta or Egypt.

29. Sea-going Service

(i) The qualification for army personnel posted for duty in sea-going vessels (para. 7). subject to the rule relating to "casual entry", will be sea-going service:—

   (a) in the Mediterranean sea East of the Straits of Gibraltar at any time between the 10th June, 1940 and 12th May, 1943, inclusive; or

(b) in direct support of army operations in Abyssinia, Somaliland or Eritrea between 10th June, 1940 and 27th November, 1941; or

(c) in Merchant Navy vessels that took part in the landing on the coast of Morocco between the 8th November, 1942 and the 12th May, 1943.

(ii) (a) Service in ships based on Gibraltar will not be a qualification unless the ships were in the area of active operations in the Mediterranean.

(b) There is no condition that the 1939-45 Star should already have been earned by six months' service before the Africa Star may be awarded.

30. Clasps

A clasp to the star may be earned for approved service with the Eighth Army or the First Army or on the staff of 18 Army Group Headquarters under the conditions stated below.

(i) To qualify for the clasp " 8th Army " personnel are required to have served between 23rd October, 1942 and 12th May, 1943, either:—

(a) on the posted strength of, or attached for duty to, a formation or unit which appeared on the Order of Battle of the Eighth Army; or

(b) as a reinforcement in a forward camp in the Eighth Army area; or

(c) with the Eighth Army on duty from units or formations not appearing on the Order of Battle, as guards and escorts on convoys, or on the staffs of hospital trains which ran to the railhead .

(d) The Eighth Army rear boundary during the period 23rd October, 1942, to 12th May, 1943, was as follows:—

(Reference maps Egypt 1/500,000 Sheets 1, 2, 4 and 5.) From Coast at 488928 to all including El Hauwariya Sta 488917-Mingar Anfigia 512881-Ras Sulimaniya 520876—thence South along 520 easting grid to 520770—all excluding 473755—cross tracks 863108 (purple grid)—including Qaret Agnes 796142 (purple grid)—then West along 090 Northing grid (purple). The line described above starts from a point on the coast approximately 16 miles S.W. of the centre of Alexandria, thence it runs due South for about 6 miles, S.S.E. for 36 miles, then due South for 61 miles and S.W. for 40 miles. It then turns westwards, finally running due West on the 090 Northing grid line.

(ii) To qualify for the clasp " 1st Army " personnel are required to have served either:—

(a) in a unit or formation in Tunisia or Algeria between 8th November, 1942 and 31st December, 1942, both dates inclusive; or

(b) in a unit of formation located forward of First Army rear boundary between 1st January and 12th May, 1943, both dates inclusive; or

(c) in a unit or formation under the command of the First Army between 1st January and 12th May, 1943, including units or formations under command of First Army for local defence and administration, whether or not the unit or formation was on the First Army Order of Battle.

(d) The First Army rear boundary during the period 1st January and 12th May, 1943, was as follows:—

(Reference maps French North Africa, GSGS 4175, Sheets NJ 31 SW and SE, NJ 32-SW, NI 31-NW and NE, NI 32-NW.) Inclusive Zribet El Oued V 99—exclusive El

Ouldja R 02—inclusive PT 1834 R 23—inclusive PT 1600 R 66—inclusive La Meskiana M 90—inclusive Dj Mesloula N 03—inclusive PT 1110 N 06—inclusive Nador M 88—inclusive Ston De Nador M 89—inclusive Bourdarouah G 80—inclusive PT 308 H 21—inclusive Munier H 31—inclusive Toustain H 32—inclusive Le Tarf H 43—inclusive Lac Melah H 45.

(iii) To qualify for the clasp " North Africa 1942-43 " for service with 18 Army Group Headquarters personnel must have served on the staff of Field Marshal (then General) Sir Harold Alexander, at 18 Army Group Headquarters during the period 15th February, 1943, to 12th May, 1943, inclusive and must not already have qualified for either the 8th or 1st Army Clasp.

(iv) The award of a clasp for army service will be denoted by emblems in the form of the Arabic " 8 " for personnel of the Eighth Army, an Arabic " 1 " for personnel of the First Army, and a silver rose for the staff of 18 Army Group Headquarters. The emblem will be worn on the ribbon when the Star itself is not worn.

(v) (a) The qualification for the award of the clasp " North Africa 1942-43 " for service with the Royal Air Force is:—

(1) service in the Eastern Air Command (later redesignated the North-West African Air Forces) or Mediterranean Air Command at any time during the period 23rd October, 1942, to 12th May, 1943; or

(2) service in a unit with the Western Desert Air Force or Middle East Command stationed West of the boundary stated at (i) (d) during the period 23rd October, 1942, to 28th November, 1942 (1200 hrs.) or West of the line of the Egyptian frontier from 28th November, 1942 (1200 hrs.) to 12th May, 1943; or

(3) service as air crew in operations in support of the First and Eighth Armies, or in the cutting of Rommel's or Von Arnim's communications, or in the Defence of Malta, during the same period.

(b) The qualification for flying personnel posted or employed on air transport, or ferrying duties during the qualifying period between 23rd October, 1942 and 12th May, 1943, will be:—

(1) flights in close support of the 8th or 1st Armies; or
(2) a landing in Malta with supplies or reinforcements for the garrison.

(c) The award of this clasp for R.A.F. service will be denoted by a silver rose emblem, to be worn on the ribbon of the Africa Star when the star itself is not worn.

(vi) (a) The clasp " North Africa 1942-43 " is granted to personnel of certain Naval units specifically engaged in cutting Rommel's or Von Arnim's communications; or for service as part of the Eighth or First Armies; or to army personnel posted for duty in sea-going vessels (para. 7), for service between 23rd October, 1942 and 12th May, 1943, in:—

(1) H.M. Ships in the Mediterranean or Levant Commands specified in Admiralty Fleet Orders.
(2) Mobile beach or port parties or permanent port parties, which operated on the coast of North Africa, West of El Alamein.
(3) Landing craft employed in ferrying stores for the First Army, which operated East of Bone.
(4) Merchant Navy vessels (see Appendix C) engaged in landing troops, equipment, stores, etc., at ports or on the shores of North Africa.

(b) (1) The award of this clasp for sea-going service will be denoted by a silver rose emblem, to be worn on the ribbon of the Africa Star when the star itself is not worn.

(2) Personnel who served on land, however, as part of the Eighth or First Armies will be awarded the clasp "Eighth Army" or the clasp "First Army" as the case may be, and will wear the appropriate emblem (but not the silver rose) on the ribbon.

Note.—Only one clasp, or emblem denoting the clasp, will be granted to any individual. In the event of double or treble qualifications, the clasp will be granted for the army or headquarters or service in which the individual first qualified, and the appropriate emblem will be worn on the ribbon.

THE PACIFIC STAR

31. General

The Pacific Star is granted for operational service in the Pacific theatre between the 8th December, 1941 and the 2nd September, 1945, inclusive, and also for certain specified service in China, Hong-Kong and Malaya.

Land Service

(i) The qualification for army personnel for service on land is entry as part of the establishment into operational service in an area defined in para. 32.

(ii) The undermentioned paid full-time members of colonial military forces, militarized police and militarized civilian bodies are eligible to qualify for the Pacific Star for operational service during the periods shown:—

	From	To
Borneo Guerilla Forces	8.12.41	3. 4.42
British North Borneo.		
Brunei.		
Labuan.		
Sarawak.		
(Local permanent resident civilians organized by Officers of Force 136 or S.R.D.)		
British Solomon Islands Defence Force	1. 2.42	30. 6.43
Gilbert and Ellice Islands Defence Force	10.12.43	4.12.43
Hong-Kong—		
Police		
Police Reserve	8.12.41	25.12.41
Special Constabulary		
Malaya—		
Malayan Guerillas	8.12.41	25. 2.42
(Enrolled guerillas under the command of Officers of Force 136.)		
Malaya Regiment	8.12.41	15. 2.42

Malayan Defence Forces 8.12.41 15. 2.42
(Federated Malay States Volunteer Force.)
Johore Volunteer Force.
Johore Volunteer Engineers.
Johore Military Force.
Kedah Volunteer Force.
Kelantan Volunteer Force.
Straits Settlements Volunteer Force.)

Malayan Police 8.12.41 15. 2.42
(Federated Malay States Police.
Johore State Police.
Johore State Wharf Police Constabulary.
Kedah State Police.
Kedah Special Force.
Kelantan State Military Police.
Perlis State Police.
Singapore Police Reserve.
Straits Settlements Police.
Trengganu State Police.)

Local Defence Corps 8.12.41 15. 2.42
(Federated Malay States and Straits Settlements.)
Malacca.
Negri Sembilan.
Pahang and Johore.
Penang.
Perak.
Singapore.

Ocean Island Defence Force 8.12.41 26. 2.42

32. Qualifying Land Areas

The land qualifying areas for the Pacific Star are:—

	From	To
(i) China	11.12.41	15. 2.42
Hong-Kong	8.12.41	25.12.41
Malaya	8.12.41	15. 2.42
Sumatra	14. 2.42	23. 3.42

(ii) (a) All Islands* in the Central Pacific and the South China Sea which were subject to enemy invasion or occupation within the area bounded on the North by Latitude 40° North and on the East by the 180th meridian. The Southern boundary of the area runs along Latitude 12° South from the 180th meridian to Longitude 145° East. The boundary then turns North along Longitude 145° East to Latitude 9° 40′ South. It runs Westward along this line to Timor. It then turns due South to Latitude 12° South, runs along this Westwards to the Longitude 110° and then to Christmas Island (excluding the Island). The boundary then runs Northwards round the South-East coast of Sumatra to Singapore.

Note.—Service in China and Malaya on or after 16th February, 1942, or Hong-Kong on or after 26th December, 1941, or in Sumatra on or after 24th March, 1942, is a qualification for the Burma Star.

---

* The Phoenix, the Samoa, the Fiji, the New Hebrides, the Cocos/Keeling and the New Caledonia Islands are not qualifying areas.

(b) The principal Islands and groups of Islands with overall qualifying dates are:—

	From	To
Bismarck Archipelago	22. 1.42	2. 9.45
British North Borneo, Brunei, Sarawak and Dutch Borneo.	*8.12.41	2. 9.45
Caroline Islands	8.12.41	2. 9.45
Celebes	†26. 1.42	2. 9.45
Gilbert and Ellice Islands	10.12.41	2. 9.45
Guam	12.12.41	2. 9.45
Iwo Jima	8.12.41	2. 9.45
Java	†5. 3.42	2. 9.45
Marianas	8.12.41	2. 9.45
Marshall Islands	8.12.41	2. 9.45
Molucca Islands	†30. 1.42	2. 9.45
Nauru	8.12.41	2. 9.45
New Guinea	7. 3.42	2. 9.45
Ocean Island	8.12.41	2. 9.45
Okinawa	8.12.41	2. 9.45
Philippine Islands	10.12.41	2. 9.45
Solomon Islands (British Solomon Islands Protectorate and Australian Mandated Territory).	1. 2.42	2. 9.45
Timor	†20. 2.42	2. 9.45
Wake Island	22.12.41	2. 9.45

Notes.

(a) Service in territories and islands shown in para. 15 (iv) qualifies for the Pacific Star in addition to the special award of the 1939-45 Star.

(b) The conditions for a special award of the Pacific Star for 30 days' service in the qualifying area on visits, journeys and inspections are stated in Section I.

33. Airborne Service

(i) Airborne troops of the army who have taken part in airborne operations in a qualifying army area will qualify by "entry into operational service."

(ii) Aircrew who flew over the qualifying land and sea areas within the dates specified, or in operations in the Aleutian Islands between the 3rd June, 1942 and the 16th August, 1943 (inclusive), will qualify by an operational sortie.

(iii) Non-Aircrew service on land qualifies under conditions laid down in para. 31 (i).

(iv) The qualification for flying personnel posted or employed on air transport or ferrying duties will be at least three landings in any of the qualifying areas shown in para. 32 during the stipulated dates.

34. Sea-going Service

(i) The qualification for army personnel posted for duty in sea-going vessels (para. 7) in direct or close support (*i.e.*, within visual contact) of land operations is "entry into operational service" as for service on land.

---

* 11.1.42 for Australian Military Forces.
† 17.12.41 for Air Transport and Ferrying Service.

(ii) (a) For other service afloat "entry into operational service" is subject to the qualification that the 1939-45 Star had previously been qualified for by 180 days' operational service.

(b) "Casual entry" into the qualifying area, e.g., in ships of the East Indies Station that crossed the Western boundary of the area for the purpose of fuelling, etc., in Western Australia will not be a qualification.

Note.—The qualifying conditions for special award of this star are stated in Section I.

(iii) *Last six months.*—Personnel who entered operational service in the qualifying area on or after the 7th March, 1945, and did not thereafter serve in the area qualifying for the Burma Star (subject to the rule as to "casual entry"), may qualify for the Pacific Star by "entry into operational service" and the six months' time qualification is waived. In such cases, except for a special award under paragraph 10 (i), the 1939-45 Star may not be awarded for service of less than 180 days.

35. Qualifying Sea Areas

The qualifying sea areas for the award of the Pacific Star are the Pacific Ocean (including the South China Sea) and the Indian Ocean East of a line running due South from Singapore round the South-East coast of Sumatra, through Christmas Island, and Southwards along the meridian of 110° East.

36. Clasp (Alternative Award)

(i) The Pacific Star and the Burma Star are alternative awards. Personnel whose service qualified for both the Pacific and the Burma Stars will be awarded only the campaign star for which they *first* qualified. They will, however, be awarded a clasp to show that they rendered service which qualified for the second star.

(ii) A silver rose emblem, denoting the award of the clasp, will be worn on the ribbon of the campaign star awarded when the star itself is not worn.

THE BURMA STAR

37. General

The Burma Star is granted for operational service in the Burma Campaign between the 11th December, 1941, and the 2nd September, 1945, and also for certain specified service in China, Malaya and Sumatra.

Land Service

(i) The qualification for army personnel for service on land is entry as part of the establishment into operational service in the area defined in para. 38.

(ii) The undermentioned categories are eligible to qualify for the Burma Star for operational service during the periods shown:—

	From	To
British Army Aid Groups, South-China (Full-time *bona fide* civilian agents employed in operational subversive activities).	16. 2.42	2. 9.45
Burma Irregular Forces (Enrolled guerillas under the command of officers of Force 136).	11.12.41	2. 9.45
Malayan Guerillas (Enrolled guerillas under the command of officers of Force 136).	16. 2.42	2. 9.45

38. Qualifying Land Areas

The qualifying areas for the Burma Star are:—

	From	To
Burma	11.12.41	2. 9.45
Bengal and Assam	1. 5.42	31.12.43
Bengal and Assam (East of the Brahmaputra and Dihang Rivers).	1. 1.44	2. 9.45
China	16. 2.42	2. 9.45
Hong-Kong	26.12.41	2. 9.45
Malaya	16. 2.42	2. 9.45
Sumatra	24. 3.42	2. 9.45

Notes.

(*a*) Service in China on or after 11th December, 1941, to 15th February, 1942, or in Malaya on or after 8th December, 1941, to 15th February, 1942, or in Sumatra on or after 14th February, 1942, to 23rd March, 1942, is a qualification for the Pacific Star.

(*b*) Service in the operations shown in para. 15 (iii)—other than in the North-West Frontier Province of India or in Malaya—qualifies for the Burma Star in addition to the special award of the 1939-45 Star.

(*c*) The conditions for a special award of the Burma Star for 30 days' service in the qualifying area on visits, journeys and inspections are stated in Section I.

39. Airborne Service

(i) Airborne troops of the army who have taken part in airborne operations in a qualifying army area for land operations qualify by entry into operational service.

(ii) Aircrew who flew over the qualifying land and sea areas within the dates specified qualify by an operational sortie.

(iii) Non-aircrew service on land qualifies under the conditions laid down in paragraph 37.

(iv) The qualification for flying personnel posted or employed on transport or ferrying duties in the air will be at least three landings in any of the qualifying areas shown in sub-para. 38 during the stipulated dates.

40. Sea-going Service

(i) The qualification for army personnel posted for duty in sea-going vessels (para. 7) in direct or close support (*i.e.*, within visual contact) of land operations is " entry into operational service " as for land service.

(ii) (*a*) For other service afloat, " entry into operational service " is subject to the qualification that the 1939-45 Star has previously been qualified for by 180 days' operational service.

(*b*) Casual entry into the qualifying area, *e.g.*, service in ships proceeding from Colombo to Trincomalee in order to refit, will not be a qualification.

Note.—The qualifying conditions for a special award of this star are stated in Section I.

(iii) *Last six months.*—Personnel who entered operational service in the qualifying sea area on, or after, the 7th March, 1945, and did not thereafter serve in the area qualifying for the Pacific Star (subject to the rule as to " casual entry ") may qualify for the Burma Star by " entry into operational service " and the six months' time qualification is waived. In such cases, except for a special award under para. 10 (i), the 1939-45 Star may not be awarded for service of less than 180 days.

41. Qualifying Sea Areas

The qualifying sea areas for the award of the Burma Star are the Bay of Bengal enclosed by a line running from the Southernmost point of Ceylon for a distance of 300 miles South thence to a point 300 miles West of the Southernmost point of Sumatra and continuing East to the Western side of Sunda Strait. The Malacca Strait is included.

42. Clasp (Alternative Award)

(i) The Burma Star and the Pacific Star are alternative awards. Personnel whose service qualified for both the Burma and the Pacific Stars, will be awarded only the campaign star for which they *first* qualified. They will, however, be awarded a clasp to show that they rendered service which qualified for the second star.

(ii) A silver rose emblem denoting the award of the clasp will be worn on the ribbon of the campaign star awarded, when the star itself is not worn.

THE ITALY STAR

43. General

The Italy Star is granted for operational service in Sicily or in Italy from the capture of Pantellaria on 11th June, 1943, until 8th May, 1945, inclusive. This star is also granted for certain operations in Sardinia, Greece, Corsica, Elba, Yugoslavia, the Aegean and Dodecanese.

Land Service

The qualification for army personnel for service on land is entry as part of the establishment into operational service in the areas defined in para. 44.

Note.—The conditions for a special award of the Italy Star for 30 days' service in the qualifying area on visits, journeys and inspections, are stated in Section I.

44. Qualifying Land Areas

The qualifying areas for the Italy Star are:—

	From	*To*
Aegean	11. 6.43	8. 5.45
Corsica	11. 6.43	4.10.43
Dodecanese	11. 6.43	8. 5.45
Greece	11. 6.43	8. 5.45
Italy (including Elba)	11. 6.43	8. 5.45
Pantellaria	11. 6.43	—
Sardinia	11. 6.43	19. 9.43
Sicily	11. 6.43	17. 8.43
Yugoslavia	11. 6.43	8. 5.45

Note.—Army personnel who entered Austrian Territory during the closing stages of hostilities in Europe are eligible for the Italy Star, but not for the France and Germany Star.

45. Airborne Service

(i) Airborne troops of the Army who have taken part in airborne operations in a qualifying army area will qualify by "entry into operational service."

(ii) Aircrew who flew on operations against the enemy in the Mediterranean Theatre of war or over Europe from bases in the Mediterranean area will qualify by an operational sortie. The Italy Star may not be awarded to air crew based elsewhere than in the Mediterranean area.

(iii) Non-aircrew service on land qualifies under para. 43.

(iv) The qualification for flying personnel posted or employed on air transport or ferrying duties will be at least three landings in any of the qualifying areas shown in para. 44 during the stipulated dates.

Flights to Europe from bases in the Mediterranean area during the period from 11th July, 1943, to 8th May, 1945, will be a qualification for the Italy Star and *not* for the France and Germany Star.

46. Sea-going Service

(i) The qualification for army personnel posted for duty in sea-going vessels (para. 7) in direct or close support (*i.e.*, within visual contact) of land operations is " entry into operational service " as for service on land, *e.g.*, service in vessels landing troops, stores, etc., at ports in or on the shores of an operational area in the Mediterranean, including Cretan and Albanian waters, or in naval operations during the invasion of the South of France.

(ii) (*a*) For other service afloat, " entry into operational service " is subject to the qualification that the 1939-45 Star has previously been qualified for by 180 days' operational service.

(*b*) " Casual entry " into the qualifying sea areas, for instance, in ships on passage through or working up, in the Mediterranean, or service in ships based on Gibraltar, North African, Palestinian and Cypriot ports not directly connected with actual operations, or service in Merchant Navy vessels landing troops, stores, etc., at ports in North Africa, Palestine, Syria and in Cyprus, or service in vessels at ports in Spain, the Balearic Islands and Turkey (East of 30° East) will *not* be regarded as service qualifying for the Italy Star.

Note.—The qualifying conditions for the " special award " of this star are stated in Section I.

(iii) *Last six months.*—Personnel who entered operational service in the qualifying area on or after the 10th November, 1944, and did not thereafter serve in any other area of active operations (subject to the rule as to casual entry) may qualify for the Italy Star, by " entry into operational service," and the necessity for the prior award of the 1939-45 Star is waived. In such cases, except for a special award under paragraph 10 (i), the 1939-45 Star may not be awarded for service of less than 180 days.

47. Qualifying Sea Areas

The qualifying sea areas for the award of the Italy Star are the Mediterranean Command, the Aegean, and Albanian and Cretan Waters.

Note.—Service in Naval operations during the invasion of the South of France is *not* a qualification for the France and Germany Star.

THE FRANCE AND GERMANY STAR

48. General

The France and Germany Star is granted for operational service in France, Belgium, Holland and Germany between the 6th June, 1944 and the 8th May, 1945, inclusive.

Land Service

(i) The qualification for army personnel is entry as part of the establishment into operational service in the area defined in para. 49.

Note.—The conditions for a special award of the France and Germany Star for 30 days' service in the qualifying area on visits, journeys and inspections are stated in Section I.

49. Qualifying Land Areas

The qualifying areas are:—

> France
> Belgium
> Luxembourg   } 6.6.44.   8.5.45.
> Holland
> Germany

Note.—Army personnel who entered Austria may *not* qualify for this award, as their service is recognized by the grant of the Italy Star.

50. Airborne Service

(i) Airborne troops of the army (para. 6) who have taken part in airborne operations will qualify by "entry into operational service."

(ii) Aircrew who flew on operations against the enemy over Europe or over the sea area (para. 52) in direct support of land operations, will qualify by one operational sortie. Other operations at sea and sorties from the Mediterranean area will *not* qualify.

(iii) Non-aircrew service on land qualifies under para. 48.

(iv) The qualification for flying personnel posted or employed on air transport or ferrying duties will be three landings in Europe from bases in the United Kingdom. Flights to Europe from bases in the Mediterranean area will be a qualification for the Italy Star and *not* for the France and Germany Star.

51. Sea-going Service

(i) The qualification for army personnel posted for duty in sea-going vessels (para. 7) in direct or close support (*i.e.*, within visual contact) of land operations is "entry into operational service," as for service on land, *e.g.*, service in Merchant Navy vessels transporting troops, stores, etc., in connection with operations.

(ii) "Casual entry" into the qualifying sea area will *not* be a qualification.

52. Qualifying Sea Areas

The qualifying sea area is the North Sea South of a line from the Firth of Forth to Kristiansand (South), in the English Channel and in the Bay of Biscay East of Longitude 6° West, provided such service was directly in support of land operations in France, Belgium, Holland or Germany.

53. Clasp (Alternative Award)

(i) Personnel qualifying for the France and Germany Star, the Atlantic Star or the Air Crew Europe Star, or two of these stars, will be awarded only the campaign star for which they *first* qualified. They will, however, be awarded a clasp to show that they rendered qualifying service for a second star. A further clasp will not be awarded to those who rendered service which would have qualified for the third star.

(ii) A silver rose emblem, denoting the clasp, will be worn on the ribbon of the campaign star awarded when the star itself is not worn.

(iii) Personnel who made air sorties against targets on land and at sea (para. 21) from the same unit do not thereby qualify for both the France and Germany Star and the Atlantic Star. In such cases the star appropriate to the normal function of the unit at the material time will be awarded *without* a clasp, except when the latter has been earned by other service. Cases of difficulty in applying this rule will be referred to the War Office (A.G. 4 Medals) for decision, before an award is made.

THE DEFENCE MEDAL

54. General

The Defence Medal is granted for non-operational service in the Armed Forces, the Home Guard, the Civil Defence Services and other approved civilian service during the period 3rd September, 1939, to 2nd September, 1945 (inclusive).

Army Qualifications

(i) The qualification for army personnel is:—
- (a) Three years' service in the United Kingdom (if normally resident therein), or three months' (90 days) service in a Mine and Bomb Disposal Unit. Military service in the United Kingdom qualifies up to 8th May, 1945.
- (b) Six months' (180 days) service overseas from or outside the country of residence in a non-operational area subjected to air attack or closely threatened. A list of the non-operational areas that were subjected to air attack or closely threatened together with the qualifying periods is given in para. 55. Service will be reckonable from the date of embarkation and will be counted at half the actual time of the voyage to the area.
- (c) One year's (360 days) service overseas from or outside the country of residence in a non-operational area other than those stated in para. 55. Military service overseas from the United Kingdom qualifies up to 2nd September, 1945. Service will be reckonable from the date of embarkation and will be counted at its full rate for the voyage to the non-operational area.
- (d) If the normal country of residence of army personnel was overseas from the United Kingdom the qualifying period for service in that country will be that laid down for full-time service with the local eligible categories in the areas defined in para. 59.

(ii) The time qualification for uniformed personnel of the classes referred to in para. 9 (iii) for service in the United Kingdom will be as for army personnel in para. 54 (i) (a).

Note.—The conditions for special awards of the Defence Medal are stated in Section I.

(iii) In dealing with claims relating to service outside the country of residence, the following territories are classified as one area; that is to say, movements by personnel from one territory to another within the defined groups will not be regarded, for the award of the Defence Medal, as " outside the country of residence," viz.:—
- (a) Great Britain, Northern Ireland, Eire, Isle of Man and the Channel Islands (including all the islands adjacent to Great Britain).
- (b) Cyprus, Syria, Lebanon, Palestine, Egypt and Transjordan.

(c) Kenya, Tanganyika, Uganda, Nyasaland, Northern Rhodesia and Zanzibar.

(d) Nigeria, Gambia, Sierra Leone and the Gold Coast.

(e) The Union of South Africa, South-West Africa, Basutoland, Swaziland and the Bechuanaland Protectorate.

Note.—Civil Defence Service in Guernsey and service in the Jersey Volunteer Force in June, 1940, is not service qualifying for the Defence Medal.

55. Threatened, etc., Areas

The territories classified as non-operational areas subjected to enemy air attack or closely threatened are:—

	From	To
(i) *Europe.*		
United Kingdom	3. 9.39	8. 5.45
(ii) *Mediterranean Area.*		
Anglo-Egyptian Sudan	3. 9.39	9. 6.40
	28.11.41	8. 5.45
Corsica	5.10.43	8. 5.45
Cyprus	3. 9.39	8. 5.45
Egypt	3. 9.39	9. 6.40
	13. 5.43	8. 5.45
Gibraltar	3. 9.39	8. 5.45
Malta	3. 9.39	9. 6.40
	13. 5.43	8. 5.45
North Africa	13. 5.43	8. 5.45
Palestine	3. 9.39	8. 5.45
Sardinia	20. 9.43	8. 5.45
Sicily	18. 8.43	8. 5.45
Sinai	3. 9.39	8. 5.45
Syria and Lebanon	3. 9.39	7. 6.41
	12. 7.41	8. 5.45
Pantellaria	12. 6.43	8. 5.45
(iii) *Indian Ocean.*		
Aden	3. 9.39	8. 5.45
Andaman Islands	3. 9.39	22. 3.42
Bengal and Assam (West of the Brahmaputra).	1. 1.44	2. 9.45
Ceylon	3. 9.39	8. 5.45
Cocos/Keeling Islands	3. 9.39	2. 9.45
Iraq	3. 9.39	9. 4.41
	1. 6.41	8. 5.45
Maldive Islands	3. 9.39	8. 5.45
Mauritius	3. 9.39	8. 5.45
Nicobar Islands	3. 9.39	22. 3.42
Persia	3. 9.39	24. 8.41
	29. 8.41	8. 5.45
Rodriquez Island	3. 9.39	2. 9.45
Seychelles	3. 9.39	8. 5.45

		From	To
(iv) *Pacific Area.*			
British North Borneo	... ...	3. 9.39	30.12.41
Brunei	... ...	3. 9.39	7.12.41
Christmas Island	... ...	3. 9.39	2. 9.45
Cook Island ...	... ...	3. 9.39	2. 9.45
Fanning Island	... ...	3. 9.39	2. 9.45
Fiji Islands ...	... ...	3. 9.39	2. 9.45
Hong-Kong ...	... ...	3. 9.39	7.12.41
Malaya	... ...	3. 9.39	7.12.41
New Caledonia ...	... ...	3. 9.39	2. 9.45
New Hebrides ...	... ...	3. 9.39	2. 9.45
Northern Territory of Australia (North of latitude 14° 30′ South).		3. 9.39	2. 9.45
Norfolk Island ...	... ...	3. 9.39	2. 9.45
Phœnix Islands	... ...	3. 9.39	2. 9.45
Rarotonga Island	... ...	3. 9.39	2. 9.45
Sarawak ...	... ...	3. 9.39	7.12.41
Tonga Island ...	... ...	3. 9.39	2. 9.45
Torres Strait Islands ...	... ...	3. 9.39	2. 9.45
Union Island ...	... ...	3. 9.39	2. 9.45
Washington Island	... ...	3. 9.39	2. 9.45
Western Samoa	... ...	3. 9.39	2. 9.45
(v) *West Atlantic.*			
Falkland Islands	... ...	3. 9.39	8. 5.45

56. Local Commissions and Recruitment Overseas

(i) (*a*) The qualification for British subjects who were living more or less permanently in the non-operational territory overseas in which they were commissioned or enlisted for service in the British Army or in the local military force (such territory being subjected to air attack or closely threatened) (para. 55) and who did not thereafter serve elsewhere, will be three years, or that laid down for the particular area as defined in para. 59.

(*b*) The qualification for those who afterwards served in a non-operational area outside the country of residence (subject to para. 54 (iii)) will be six months in an area closely threatened, etc. (para. 55) or one year elsewhere as for army personnel.

(*c*) Those who were living more or less permanently in a non-operational territory neither subjected to air attack nor closely threatened and did not serve elsewhere (*e.g.*, officers commissioned in America for duty with the British Army Staff or personnel of the local forces in West Africa or the West Indies), may not count such service as a qualification for the Defence Medal. (They will, however, be eligible for the War Medal, 1939-45).

(*d*) Those who left the territory of residence (*e.g.*, from the Argentine Republic to the United Kingdom), will qualify on entering military service in the United Kingdom or in a similar qualifying area.

(*e*) Cases of difficulty in applying the above rules will be referred to the War Office (A.G. 4 (Medals)) for decision. Consideration will be given to applications from individuals who were not normally resident in the territory in which they joined the armed forces after 3rd September, 1939, but who were there on a temporary visit and did not relinquish their previous domicile elsewhere.

(ii) *Indian Army.*

Indian Army personnel referred to in para. 70 are not permitted to count service in *India* for the Defence Medal, as such service qualifies for the India Service Medal, 1939-45.

57. Home Guard

(i) The qualification for enrolled members of the Home Guard (para. 9) and personnel of specified units of the Territorial Army Reserve before embodiment, is:—

    (a) Three years' part-time service in the United Kingdom (or three months' (90 days) service in mine and bomb disposal units) from 14th May, 1940, to 31st December, 1944 (inclusive); or,

    (b) Six months' (180 days) for British Commonwealth citizens from overseas who served in the Home Guard in the United Kingdom.

Note.—The conditions for a special award of this Medal are stated in Section I, para. 10.

58. Approved Civilian Categories

The qualification for the specially approved categories of civilians (para. 9 (i)), who were eligible to qualify for campaign stars for service with the armed forces, is six months' (180 days) service *overseas from, or outside,* the normal country of residence in a non-operational territory subjected to enemy air attack or closely threatened during the qualifying periods as shown in paras. 54 (iii) and 55. Service in the United Kingdom and service in transit to a scheduled non-operational area, may not be reckoned as qualifying service.

59. Colonial Empire and Mandated Territories

Service in the country of residence by members of colonial local military forces or militarized civilian bodies and other special categories of civilians in a qualifying territory for the Defence Medal, may be reckoned towards the required time qualification for this award, but any service rendered which qualifies for the grant of campaign stars will not reckon towards the Defence Medal.

The eligible categories with their respective qualifying periods and qualifying dates are shown below:—

Local Military Force	Time Qualification	From	To
(i) *Mediterranean Area*			
Cyprus			
Volunteer Force	Three years	15. 6.40	8. 5.45
Gibraltar			
Defence Force	Three years	3. 9.39	8. 5.45
Malta			
Local Military Forces	Two years	3. 9.39 13. 5.43	9. 6.40 8. 5.45
Home Guard (M.V.D.F.)		3. 9.39	8. 5.45
(Note.—Service in the Auxiliary Corps is not a qualification).			
Palestine			
Volunteer Force	One year and six months	12. 5.41	8. 5.45
Police	One year and six months	27. 5.42	8. 5.45
Sudan (Anglo Egyptian)			
(a) Defence Force			
Full time permanent staff anywhere in the Sudan.	Three years	3. 9.39 28.11.41	9. 6.40 8. 5.45

Local Military Force	Time Qualification	From	To
(b) Police (including Provincial and Railway police)			
Full time or part-time paid service in the Sudan as part of the Sudan Defence Force.	Three years	3. 9.39 / 28.11.41	9. 6.40 / 8. 5.45
Part-time service in areas specified in para. 27 (ii).	90 days	10. 6.40	27.11.41
(c) Auxiliary Defence Force			
Full time members who commanded Sudan Police or other military personnel in a unit earning campaign stars.	Three years	3. 9.39 / 28.11.41	9. 6.40 / 8. 5.45
Enrolled Volunteers			
Full or part-time service anywhere in the Sudan.	Three years	3. 9.39 / 28.11.41	9. 6.40 / 8. 5.45
Part-time service of uniformed, armed and trained personnel in areas specified in para. 27 (ii).	90 days	10. 6.40	27.11.41
*A.A. Companies, Sudan Auxiliary Defence Force			
If uniformed, armed and trained, full or part-time service anywhere in the Sudan.	Three years	3. 9.39 / 28.11.41	9. 6.40 / 8. 5.45
A.A. Companies, S.A.D.F. No. 1 at Khartoum. No. 2 at Atbara. No. 3 at Port Sudan. No. 4 at Khartoum North (Steamers Dept.). No. 5 in Stores and Ordnance Depts.	90 days	10. 6.40	27.11.41
(ii) *Indian Ocean*			
Aden			
Home Guard	Two year nine months.	June, 1941	3.12.44
Levies	Two year nine months.	June, 1941	3.12.44
Ceylon			
Colombo Town Guard	Three years	6. 9.39	1. 1.45
Mauritius			
Defence Force	One year six months.	30.12.41	31.12.44
Home Guard			
Volunteer Air Force			
Seychelles			
Defence Force	Two years	3. 9.39	31.12.44
Pioneer Corps			

	Local Military Force	Time Qualification	From	To
(iii)	*Pacific Area*			
	British North Borneo, Brunei and Sarawak.			
	Police and Special Police.	} One day	8.12.41	3. 4.42
	Constabulary and Armed Constabulary.			
	Rangers and Volunteer Force.			
	Fiji			
	Defence Force	} Three years	3. 9.39	2. 9.45
	Home Guard			
	Reserve Company			
	Fire Service (Permanent Staff)			
	Hong Kong			
	Volunteer Defence Corps ...	One year...	3. 9.39	7.12.41
	~~Local Defence Force~~	~~One year...~~	~~3. 9.39~~	~~7.12.41~~
	Medical Auxiliary Service ...	One day ...	8.12.41	25.12.41
	Malaya			
	Malay Regiment	One year...	3. 9.39	7.12.41
	Malayan Armed Forces (*full or part-time service*)			
	Federated Malay States, V.F.	} One year...	3. 9.39	7.12.41
	Johore Volunteer Force ...			
	Johore Volunteer Engineers			
	Johore Military Force ...			
	Kedah Volunteer Force			
	Kelantan Volunteer Force ...			
	Straits Settlements, V.F. ...			
	Malay Medical Auxiliary Service.	One day ...	8.12.41	15. 2.42
	Local Defence Corps (Federated Malay States and Straits Settlements)			
	Malacca	} One year ...	3. 9.39	7.12.41
	Negri Sembilan			
	Pahang and Johore... ...			
	Penang			
	Perak			
	Singapore			
	(*Part-time or full-time service*)			
	Singapore			
	Medical Auxiliary Service ...	} One day ...	8.12.41	15. 2.42
	Civilians in Military Establishments.			
	Rarotonga			
	Defence Force	Eighteen months.	1. 1.41	7.10.43
	Tonga			
	Defence Force	Three years	3. 9.39	4.12.44
	Western Samoa			
	Local Defence Force (Permanent Force) (*service with the L.D.F. Reserve is not a qualification*).	Three years	3. 9.39	2. 9.45

Local Military Force	Time Qualification	From	To
(iv) West Atlantic Falkland Islands Defence Force ... South Georgia Defence Force.	Three years	3. 9.39	8. 5.45

60. Foreign Subjects

(i) (a) Poles who served in the United Kingdom as part of the Polish Forces, are eligible for the Defence Medal, on the same terms as members of the United Kingdom Forces (para. 54).

(b) Poles who served overseas from the United Kingdom in non-operational areas in units under British command are eligible for the Defence Medal on the same terms as United Kingdom Forces (para. 54).

(c) Poles who served under British command in a non-operational area overseas from the United Kingdom, but who did not serve at any time in the United Kingdom, are eligible to qualify for the Defence Medal on the same terms as those Poles who went overseas from the United Kingdom, and will be treated as though the United Kingdom had been their normal country of residence (para. 54).

(ii) Members of W.T.S./F.A.N.Y. who served as civilians with the Polish Forces under British command overseas from the United Kingdom in non-operational areas which were subjected to enemy air attack or closely threatened (para. 55) are eligible to qualify for the Defence Medal as in sub-para. (i) above.

61. Civilians—United Kingdom

(i) The qualification for members of civilian services in the United Kingdom eligible for chevrons for war service, whether part-time or whole-time, during the period the enrolled member was available for duty up to the standard required from time to time, and performed such duty as and when required (in no case being less than 48 hours monthly), is three years from 3rd September, 1939, to 8th May, 1945, or whatever earlier date may have been fixed for the cessation of service in particular cases. A list of civilian categories serving in the United Kingdom eligible for chevrons for war service and the Defence Medal is shown at Appendix D. (The procedure for the administration of awards to eligible civilians employed in War Department premises is laid down in A.C.I. 613 of 1946.) *Note.*—Civil Defence Service in the Channel Islands is *not* a qualification for the Defence Medal.

(ii) Members of the Joint War Organization of the British Red Cross Society and the Order of St. John, the Scottish Branch of the British Red Cross Society and the St. Andrew's Ambulance Association can qualify as above if (a) they were enrolled in an eligible local authority Civil Defence Service, or (b) they performed duties analogous to those of one of the eligible local authority Civil Defence Service (in no case less than 48 hours each month) and the section of the organization to which they belonged was one which functioned operationally during, or immediately after, enemy attacks. (Administration will be by the Home Office, except for those referred to in para. 58, in accordance with the instructions given in Civil Form D.M. 1).

(iii) (a) *Civil Defence Services (United Kingdom)*
The terminal date for full-time Civil Defence Services is 8th May, 1945.
(b) *National Fire Service*
The terminal date for full-time National Fire Service is 8th May, 1945. Part-time members of the N.F.S. who were no longer required for regular duty after 15th December, 1944 (England and Wales) or after 19th January, 1945 (Scotland) but desired to retain their connections with the Service and

were " stood down " on the understanding that they would report for duty if required, will be entitled to count such service up to 8th May, 1945, towards the qualifying period.

(c) Fire Guards

The terminal date for qualifying service will be the date of de-prescription of the area or the 8th May, 1945, whichever was the earlier. The London Civil Defence Region and in *large cities* and many *smaller towns* in Civil Defence Regions (1), (7), (8), (9), (10) and in substantial parts of Regions (2) North-Eastern, (3) North Midland and (6) Southern, de-prescription was effected on 30th April, 1945. In Scotland, de-prescription was completed by 26th March, 1945. No fire guard service will be reckoned in any area subsequent to de-prescription of the area.

(d) Canteen (etc.) Services

Members of categories 11, 12, 13, 14 and 15 of Appendix D will qualify only where they have been engaged in a section of the service which had, or would have had, operational functions during or immediately after enemy attacks, and were thus engaged on service which was qualifying service for war service (red) chevrons.

62. Civil Defence Organizations—Overseas

(i) Civil Defence service in military operational areas (as defined under the appropriate campaign stars) or in non-operational areas subjected to enemy air attack will qualify for the Defence Medal, provided the civil category was not eligible for campaign stars and the service was rendered during the qualifying period laid down for the particular area.

(ii) Awards in respect of such service will be administered by the local authority concerned.

Note.—Civil Defence Service in the territory of residence neither subjected to enemy air attack nor closely threatened, *e.g.,* in West Africa or the West Indies will not be a qualification for the Defence Medal.

63. Emblem

The conditions for the award of the emblem of silver laurel leaves in respect of the grant of a King's Commendation for service as a civilian (other than for service in the Merchant Navy), are laid down in Army Order 109 of 1947.

THE WAR MEDAL 1939-45

64. General

The War Medal 1939-45 is granted for *full-time* service in the Armed Forces and Merchant Navy during the period 3rd September, 1939, to 2nd September, 1945, inclusive.

Army Qualifications

(i) The qualification for army personnel will be 28 days' service wherever rendered.

(ii) Full-time paid members of the specially approved colonial military forces, militarized police or militarized civilian bodies, eligible to qualify for campaign stars as shown in sub-paras. 14 (ii), 26 (ii), 31 (ii), 37 (ii), will also be eligible to qualify for the War Medal 1939-45 for 28 days' service during the qualifying period laid down for the force concerned.

(iii) The undermentioned paid full-time members of colonial military forces, militarized police and militarized civilian bodies are eligible to qualify for the War Medal 1939-45 by 28 days' service during the periods shown below (part-time personnel may not count periods of full-time service while training or on courses of instruction).

	From	To
British Guiana Constabulary (excluding those who ceased to belong to the Force for reasons other than death, ill-health, or age).	3. 9.39	14. 7.45
Cyprus Police Force (employed on full-time Military Service).	10. 6.40	12. 6.41
Cyprus Volunteer Force	2. 6.41	2. 9.45
Gambia Police Force	5. 7.40	17. 6.40
Gambia (Army Inland Water Transport—S.S. Munshi).	21. 7.42	31. 5.44
Gibraltar Defence Force	3. 9.39	2. 3.40
Nigeria Police Force	1940	8. 5.45
Palestine Police Force	27. 5.42	8. 5.45
Sudan Defence Force (full-time permanent service anywhere in the Sudan).	3. 9.39	8. 5.45

65. Approved Civilian Categories

The qualification for the specially approved categories of uniformed civilians (para. 9 (i)) eligible to qualify for campaign stars will be 28 days' service:—

(i) in the area of an army operational command overseas, or
(ii) overseas from or outside the country of residence in non-operational areas subjected to enemy air attack or closely threatened (para. 55).

Service in the United Kingdom or in the territory of residence (other than in an army operational area) will not be a qualification.

66. Sea-going Service

(i) Qualifying service in the Merchant Navy is 28 days' service anywhere at sea during the qualifying period.

(ii) Officers holding " time only " commissions in the R.N.V.R. (SP.) for duty with the Sea Cadet Corps are not eligible for the War Medal 1939-45, though they may have received pay for 28 days or more while attending camps and/or courses.

67. Foreign Subjects

Foreign subjects commissioned or enlisted into British Forces who do not receive a similar award to the War Medal 1939-45 from their own Governments are eligible to qualify for this medal.

Note.—The condition for the special awards of the War Medal 1939-45 are stated in Section I, para. 10.

68. Emblem

The conditions for the award and method of wearing of the oak leaf emblem in respect of a Mention in Despatches or a King's Commendation are laid down in Army Order 109 of 1947.

Note.—A citation in command, etc., orders or a certificate for good service or a lesser distinction of a similar nature is not to be regarded as a King's Commendation.

INDIA SERVICE MEDAL 1939-45

69. General

The India Service Medal 1939-45 is granted to commemorate non-operational service in the Indian Forces and Indian Civil Defence Service in India or elsewhere during the 1939-45 War. This medal will not be granted to anyone eligible for the Defence Medal.

Qualifications for Award

The qualification for personnel referred to below will be three years' non-operational service in India or elsewhere, on the authorized establishment of a unit or formation of the Indian Forces between 3rd September, 1939 and 2nd September, 1945. Service in non-operational areas elsewhere, which is not in itself sufficient to qualify for the Defence Medal, may be aggregated with non-operational service in India.

70. Indian Army Categories

Personnel eligible to qualify for the India Service Medal 1939-45 are:—

(i) *British officers on the Active List, Viceroy Commissioned officers.
  *Regular British other ranks, Indian warrant officers and Indian other ranks of the:—
   (a) Indian Army.
   (b) India unattached list (permanent cadre only).
   (c) Special unemployed list.

* *Note.*—India is officially regarded as the country of residence.

(ii) Officers, other ranks and members of the:—
   (a) Auxiliary Forces (India) (when embodied or attached to the Indian Regular Forces).
   (b) Indian Territorial Forces (when embodied or attached to the Indian Regular Forces).
   (c) Indian State Forces (serving under the Crown).
   (d) Indian Military Nursing Service.
       Auxiliary Nursing Service (India).
       Auxiliary Nursing Service Reserve.
       Women's Auxiliary Corps (India).

(iii) Enrolled non-combatants and civilians in Military employ who were:—
   (a) uniformed;
   (b) enrolled in specified military units or formation; or
   (c) were liable for general service and formed part of the authorized war establishment.

(iv) Emergency commissioned officers and British other ranks of either the British or Indian Army who *were resident in India prior to 3rd September,* 1939 and who were commissioned or recruited in India.

(v) Statutory Indians, including Europeans domiciled in India and Anglo-Indians whose country of residence is India, who rendered non-operational service in the British Military Forces in India, or elsewhere, and who are not eligible for the Defence Medal.

71. Ineligible Categories

The following categories, other than those eligible to qualify under para. 70 (iv) above, are not eligible for the India Service Medal 1939-45:—
   (i) All ranks of the United Kingdom Forces in India, including those stationed in India before 3rd September, 1939.
   (ii) Emergency commissioned officers, recruited from the United Kingdom subsequent to 2nd September, 1939.
   (iii) British other ranks in the Indian Army recruited from outside India subsequent to 2nd September, 1939.

72. Method of Application

Applications for the award of the India Service Medal by British Army personnel may be made to the War Office, A.G. 4 (Medals). All other applications will be referred to the Commonwealth Relations Office.

SECTION III
ADMINISTRATION

73. Service Personnel

Forms of Application

(i) All personnel of the United Kingdom Armed Forces and members of categories shown in para. 2 (iii), (iv) and (vi) should make a personal application for campaign stars and clasps and/or for the Defence Medal on the appropriate form and in accordance with the instructions laid down in the following paragraphs.

(ii) As the War Medal 1939-45 is automatically awarded on the completion of 28 days' full-time service in the Armed Forces, there is no special army claim form for this medal.

(iii) Claims for the India Service Medal should be made on A.I.F. Z 3014 in accordance with Army Instructions (India) No. 7-S of 10th July, 1946.

(iv) The appropriate forms for Merchant Navy service are C.R.S. 109 (Campaign stars and clasps) and C.R.S. 110 (War Medal 1939-45). These will be used only when the *last* period of qualifying service was under the Ministry of War Transport (*see* para. 78).

(v) The revised qualifying conditions for campaign stars and the Defence Medal will not necessitate the submission of a further A.F. B 2070/2068 (in the case of those who have already submitted these forms), unless details of service *now* qualifying for campaign stars or the Defence Medal have not already been shown on the claim forms previously submitted, or when the original claim form is not available.

74. Instructions for Claiming Campaign Stars

(i) *Land Service*
   (a) Army personnel claiming campaign stars should complete full details of operational service in accordance with the instructions on A.F. B 2070. Non-operational service should not be shown on this form. When a claim is made for visits, journeys and inspections, the authority for the visit and the actual dates of service in the operational area should be stated.

(b) When a claim is made for operational service after escape or liberation, documentary evidence (such as a certificate by a senior British officer who was actually in charge of and present with the party when the operational service was performed) must be produced in support of the claim (*see* para. 11 (ii) (*c*)).
(c) Those who escaped from captivity and rendered *operational* service with a fighting partisan organization should produce documentary evidence by the senior British officer who was actually in charge of the party, or if one were not present during such service, by a responsible witness who has first-hand knowledge of the service claimed (*see* para. 11 (ii) (*c*)).
(d) Applications in respect of " special " service should be submitted in accordance with para. 11 (iii).

(ii) *Airborne Service*
(a) When a claim is made for airborne service (para. 6) the air operational unit, its location (whether or not it was in a non-operational area, *e.g.*, the United Kingdom), the dates of operational service therein (*see* para. 6), full details of the operational sorties and the landing in the operational area should be stated.
(b) Personnel employed on air transportation and ferrying duties will be required to show details of three landings or three round trips.
(c) Application in respect of awards for service as civil air crew should be made to the Ministry of Civil Aviation, S.P. Division (S.P. 1), Ariel House, Strand, London, W.C. 2.

(iii) *Sea-Going Service*
When a claim is made for sea-going service (para. 7) the names of the vessels in which served, the dates of embarkation and disembarkation for each round trip or one-way trip and the sea area of active operations appropriate to the star claimed should be stated.

75. Instructions for Claiming Defence Medal

(i) *Army Qualifications*
Personnel whose most recent qualifying service was in the Army should make personal application for the Defence Medal on A.F. B 2068. Details of service in operational areas should not be shown on this form. The procedure thereafter will be as required for campaign stars.

(ii) *Mixed Service*
(a) Those who rendered previous Home Guard qualifying service and wish it to be aggregated with military service, should show full particulars on A.F. B 2068. The form should be forwarded to the Headquarters of the County Territorial and Auxiliary Forces Association for certification at Part III.
(b) Those who have had previous qualifying service in the Royal Navy or Royal Marines and wish it to be aggregated with Military or Home Guard service must show such service on A.F. B 2068. When service cannot be verified from available records, A.F. B 2068 should be forwarded to the Director of Navy Accounts, Admiralty, for completion of Part III.
(c) Those who have had previous qualifying service in the R.A.F., before transfer, or before being commissioned, or enlisted in the Army, and wish it to be aggregated with military or Home Guard

service, should show details of R.A.F. service on A.F. B 2068. When service cannot be verified from available records, the form should be forwarded to the Air Ministry (officers), or R.A.F. Record Office, Gloucester (ex-airmen), for completion of Part III.

(d) Serving members of the forces who rendered qualifying civilian service before being commissioned or enlisted and who wish to aggregate qualifying civilian service with military service, should obtain a certificate on Civil Form D.M. 3 from the civilian authorities concerned and attach it to A.F. B 2068. Supplies of the civilian forms may be obtained from the War Office, A.G. 4 (Medals), by O.C. units, etc., for individuals serving overseas. The individual, however, will be responsible for obtaining the the certificate from the authority concerned and should attach it to A.F. B 2068 for the service to be aggregated.

(e) Where certification is sought of the performance of fire guard or civil defence duty at business premises, application for the necessary certificate should *not* be made to the local authority but to the business or Government Department concerned. If Civil Form D.M. 3 is not returned within three months (six months for those overseas), application may then be made to the local authority by the individual, who should state why this is being done.

76. Instructions for Claiming India Service Medal 1939-45

Individuals making application for the India Service Medal 1939-45 should state:—

    (i) Number, rank and name.
   (ii) Normal country of residence before being commissioned or enlisted into the British Army.
  (iii) Date of being commissioned or date of transfer to the Indian Forces.
  (iv) Nature of commission:—
       (a) In the Indian Army.
       (b) In the British Army.
   (v) Dates of other rank service (if applicable) in the British Army.
  (vi) Details of dates and place of service for which the award is claimed.

77. Procedure for Verification and Disposal of Forms

The procedure for the verification and disposal of the claim forms will be as follows:—

(i) *Units not administered by a G.H.Q. 2nd Echelon*

(a) The O.C. unit will verify the service claimed from records in his possession, make an award of the star or clasp or Defence Medal where applicable and complete the appropriate certificate on the claim form.

(b) A record will be made in every instance where, but for a prior award of the star first earned, qualifying service has been rendered which would have qualified for a second or third star.

(c) The award will be published in Part II/III Orders and recorded on A.F. B 199A or A.F. B 103 and in A.B. 439 or A.B. 64, Part I.

(d) The grant of the War Medal 1939-45 will not be published in Part II/III Orders. The award will, however, be recorded on A.F. B 199A or A.F. B 103 and in A.B. 439 or A.B. 64, Part I.

(e) When qualifying service cannot be verified, or when there is doubt as to entitlement, or in any case of difficulty in applying these instructions, the claim form should be forwarded under a memorandum stating full details of the case to the War Office for officers or to the unit Records Office in the case of other ranks.

(f) Certified claim forms with the Part II/III Orders will be forwarded for documentation to the War Office (officers), or to the unit Records Office in the case of other ranks. All awards will be recorded on A.F. B 199A (original) or A.F. B 200.

(ii) *Units administered by a G.H.Q. 2nd Echelon*

The claim forms for campaign stars, clasps, or the Defence Medal of officers and other ranks will be forwarded by Os.C. units to the O. i/c G.H.Q. 2nd Echelon for verification of service, assessment of entitlement, certification, publication in Part II Orders and documentation. Subsequent action will be in accordance with that laid down in the sub-paragraphs above. Os.C. units will be responsible for the entry of awards in A.B. 439 or A.B. 64, Part I.

(iii) *General*

(a) The War Office and Os. i/c Records will be responsible for the further investigation of claims which Os.C. units or G.H.Q's. 2nd Echelon have been unable to verify. Claims subsequently authorized or rejected will be returned to the unit or formation concerned for appropriate action.

(b) No action is to be taken by units in respect of non-effective personnel previously borne on their strength. All enquiries regarding the medal entitlement of personnel who have ceased service, or of deceased and missing personnel will be referred to the War Office (officers) or the Records Office (other ranks).

Note.—Historical Records.—A schedule showing the allocation of units and formations located in operational commands has been issued to O. i/c Records or G.H.Q. 2nd Echelons for the assessment of claims. A list of units classified as air operational units will be promulgated later.

78. Transfers and Re-enlistments

(i) Campaign stars, the Defence Medal and the War Medal 1939-45 awarded for service in the Royal Navy, Royal Marines, Army, Royal Air Force, Commonwealth Forces, Colonial Forces or the Merchant Navy will be administered:—

(a) for serving personnel (including those transferred)—by the Service Department in which the individuals are now serving;

(b) for released personnel—by the service in which the individuals were serving at the time of release;

(c) for personnel who, after release, re-enlisted into a different service—by the service to which their final claims were, or should have been, submitted and which *holds the records of their service* during the 1939-45 War.

(ii) For service in the Home Guard, including *former* complete or incomplete qualifying service in the Armed Forces or in an approved civilian category, the award of the *Defence Medal* will be made by the Secretary of the Territorial and Auxiliary Forces Association of the county in which the *last* period of service was rendered.

(iii) (*a*) In the case of Royal Navy service, O. i/c Records should forward Service Certificate S. 459 with the appropriate army form to the Admiralty to advise star/medal entitlement or to confirm service which may be aggregated with other qualifying service.

(*b*) Where records of other rank service in the R.A.F. are not held, application will be made to the Air Officer i/c R.A.F. Records. If the claim is made for air crew service, the flying log book, if available, or full particulars of one or more sorties relevant to the claim, should be supplied.

(*c*) Claims for service in the Merchant Navy on Ministry of War Transport Forms C.R.S. 109 or C.R.S. 110 should be forwarded to the Registrar of Shipping and Seamen, Llantrisant Road, Llandaff, Cardiff.

Note.—Every precaution is to be taken to avoid duplication of issues by any other medal issuing authority. The branch or office dealing with the claim involving " mixed " service will notify the Government Department concerned, whether or not the stars/medals will be administered by the War Department.

79. Non-effectives
Forms of Application

Non-effective officers and ex-soldiers will be required to submit a' claim for the stars, clasps and Defence Medal to which they consider they are entitled. Application may be made to the War Office, or to a Record Office or any military establishment for an A.F. B 2070 or B 2068, or to the Home Office for the required civil forms.

80. Instructions for Claiming Campaign Stars

The procedure laid down for verification, assessment and documentation for serving personnel (except for publication in Part II Orders), will be followed. Stars, medals, ribbons and emblems will be issued as supplies become available.

81. Instructions for Claiming Defence Medal

(i) *Army qualifications*

Officers not now serving and ex-other ranks of the Army and auxiliary military services whose most recent qualifying service was rendered in the Army, may obtain A.F. B 2068 from any military establishment. The claimant, when he has entered the required particulars on the form, should send it to the War Office (officers only), or to the Records Office of the unit with which service was last rendered.

(ii) *Mixed Service*

(*a*) Those who wish to add previous qualifying service in the Royal Navy or Royal Marines to army service, should show such service on A.F. B 2068, which should be forwarded to the Director of Navy Accounts, Admiralty, for the completion of Part II and onward transmission to the War Office or to the appropriate Records Office.

(*b*) Those who wish to add previous R.A.F. qualifying service should show such service on A.F. B 2068, which should be forwarded to the Air Ministry (officers) or Air Officer i/c Records, Gloucester (other ranks), for the completion of Part III and onward transmission to the War Office, or to the appropriate Army Records Office.

(*c*) Those who rendered previous Home Guard qualifying service and wish it to be aggregated with Army service should complete A.F. B 2068 and send to the appropriate headquarters of the Territorial Army Association of the County in which service was last rendered, for completion of the certificate at Part III. On its return the form should be forwarded to the War Office or to the appropriate Records Office.

(d) Those who rendered previous qualifying civilian service and wish to aggregate it with qualifying military service, should obtain a certificate on Form D.M. 3. This will be attached to A.F. B 2068 and forwarded to the War Office or appropriate army Records Office.

(e) When certification is sought of the performance of fire guard or civil defence duty at business premises, application should *not* be made to the local authority but to the business or Government Department concerned. If a Civil Form D.M. 3 is not returned within three months (six months for army personnel overseas) application may then be made to the local authority by the individual, who should state why this is being done.

(f) Ex-service personnel who rendered qualifying *civilian* service *after* leaving the Armed Forces (including the Home Guard) and wish to aggregate earlier qualifying service in the Armed Forces, should obtain Civil Forms D.M. 2 and D.M. 4. Details of service in the Armed Forces should be shown on Form D.M. 4, which should be sent to the War Office, or to the appropriate Records Office, for certification and should then be attached to Form D.M. 2 and forwarded to the appropriate local civil authority under whom the last period of qualifying service was rendered. Personnel making a claim under these circumstances should *not* use A.F. B 2068.

82. Deceased Personnel

Stars, clasps and medals awarded to officers and other ranks who have not lived to receive them will be issued to the legal beneficiaries in accordance with King's Regulations, 1940, para. 1076.

The entitlement to and issue of campaign stars, clasps and medals will be recorded on A.F. B 199A or A.F. B 200.

Note.

Campaign stars and medals instituted during the 1939-45 War will not be stamped with the service particulars of the recipient at Government expense, nor under Government arrangements.

83. Commonwealth Forces

The administration of campaign stars, clasps and medals for Dominion, etc., personnel, including those who served with the British Army under the special loan schemes (Canloan or Southloan, etc.) or exchange schemes, will be undertaken by the Governments concerned.

Claims by Canloan or Southloan officers will be verified and certified by the War Office and the army form should be forwarded to the appropriate Dominion Government, for the issue of the stars and medals.

84. Colonial and Local Military Forces

The administration of campaign stars, clasps and medals for personnel of Colonial Forces will be undertaken by the appropriate Colonial or Local Records Office.

85. Colonial Police

The records of Occupied Enemy Territory Administration Colonial Police are maintained locally, and the local government concerned will be responsible for the administration of the award. The military commander will have arranged for the checking, recording of entitlement of awards and the issue of ribbon.

Applications by officers and other ranks of Colonial, etc., Police Forces, now serving in the Army, for awards for colonial police service will be forwarded to the War Office (A.G. 4 Medals).

86. Specially Approved Civilian Categories
Instructions for Claiming Campaign Stars

All members should make claims for campaign stars on A.F. B 2070—supplies of which may be obtained on application to the War Office. Application should be made to the Secretary (or Principal, or Chief Regional Officer in the case of Civil Defence Services), at the headquarters of the organization to which the individual belonged during the period of service in areas for which the particular campaign star is awarded, or to the War Office in the case of independent members shown at para. 9.

Note.—The expression " approved civilian organization " or " approved civilian service " means service in an organization listed at para. 9.

87. Procedure for Verification and Disposal of Forms

(i) (*a*) The secretaries of organizations will deal with all applications from members and verify the service claimed. The completed claim forms should be forwarded to the War Office for confirmation that army requirements have been satisfied. The stars, medals, and ribbons will be forwarded to the individual concerned by the War Office.

(*b*) Where a claim is disallowed, or qualifying service cannot be verified, or there is doubt as to eligibility, the claim form should be forwarded to the War Office under a memorandum stating the reason for submission; awards subsequently approved or rejected will be notified to the Secretary concerned.

(ii) *Members in military areas overseas.*

The claim forms should be forwarded to the nearest headquarters for verification of award.

When qualifying service cannot be verified, or when there is doubt as to eligibility, the claim forms should be forwarded to the War Office as in para. (i) (*b*).

All claim forms (A.F. B 2070) authorizing the awards, should be forwarded to the War Office as soon as the ribbon has been issued.

(iii) Claims by serving officers and other ranks of the Army in respect of former civilian service in any of the approved civilian organizations, should be submitted by officers commanding units to the War Office for investigation. If the service is approved, the claim form should be returned to the G.H.Q. or officer commanding unit for publication in Part II/III Orders and will thereafter be disposed of in the normal manner.

88. Instructions for Claiming Defence Medal

(i) (*a*) The verification of claims for the Defence Medal to individuals who completed the necessary qualifications will be undertaken by the secretary of the organization concerned. Where, however, and individual was subsequently commissioned or enlisted in the Army, the administration will be undertaken by the War Office for officers, or by Records Offices for other ranks.

(b) Members and ex-members of the approved civilian organizations whose most recent qualifying service was rendered as a civilian member of such organization should complete A.F. B 2068 and send it to the appropriate headquarters.

(ii) *Mixed Service*
  (a) Those who rendered qualifying civilian service before becoming members of the approved civilian organization and wish to aggregate Civil Defence, etc., service with overseas non-operational civilian service (para. 55), should obtain a certificate on Civil Form D.M. 3, and attach it to A.F. B 2068 when sending the claim to the H.Q.
  (b) Those who rendered qualifying Civil Defence service after leaving the approved civilian organization and wish to aggregate former service with Civil Defence service, should obtain Civil Form D.M. 4 and attach it to D.M. 2, when making a claim to the civil authority concerned (Appendix D).
  (c) Members who were subsequently commissioned or enlisted in the Army and are still serving and who wish approved civilian service to count as qualifying service should submit A.F. B 2068 to their Commanding Officers who will forward the claim forms to the War Office for verification.
  Those not now serving may obtain A.Fs. B 2068 from any Records Office.

(iii) Ex-members of an approved civilian organization who have had previous service with the Royal Navy, or Royal Air Force, and wish to add such service to approved civilian service, should obtain the appropriate R.N. or R.A.F. certificate from the service department concerned.

(iv) All claim forms authorizing the award of the Defence Medal should be forwarded to the War Office.

(v) V.A.D.—The procedure for the award of the Defence Medal to members of Voluntary Aid Detachments in respect of service under the Army Council with military medical establishments will be as follows:—
  (a) The War Department will administer the Defence Medal for all V.A.D. members whose last qualifying service was in a military medical establishment and who completed the required qualifying period of service before 1st January, 1944, or after enrolment under the conditions of A.C.I. 1773 of 1943. In such cases A.F. B 2068 should be completed and forwarded to the O. i/c R.A.M.C. Records for enrolled members, or to the War Office A.G. 4 (Medals) for commandants and assistant commandants whose appointments were abolished. Where military medical establishments have been disbanded, claims may be certified by the director of medical services at command headquarters.
  (b) The Home Office will administer claims for the Defence Medal (under category 20 shown on Civil Form D.M. 1) in respect of service in the United Kingdom for all members of V.A.D's., including commandants and assistant commandants, who served in military medical establishments before 1st January, 1944, but who were neither enrolled for employment under the Army Council, nor completed the required time qualification for the Defence Medal

before their services were terminated and did not thereafter serve with the armed forces or serve overseas in a specially approved civilian category eligible to qualify for campaign stars.

Those members who did not serve under the Army Council in medical establishments of the Armed Forces should obtain a certificate from the county controller, who holds the permanent records of members, that she was serving as a member of the Voluntary Aid Detachment, subsequent to 2nd September, 1939. This certificate should then be attached to either Civil Form D.M. 2, or D.M. 3 or D.M. 4 for service at the medical establishment to be certified. The forms and certificates should then be sent to the Home Office for appropriate action. Where the military medical establishment has been disbanded, the Director of Medical Services of Commands may certify Civil Form D.M. 4 at part E.

89. War Medal 1939-45

The award of this medal is automatic on the completion of 28 days' qualifying service overseas.

(i) Secretaries of organizations will be required to submit to the War Office (A.G. 4 (Medals)), a nominal roll giving the names in alphabetical order of those who have qualified for this award under the conditions laid down in para. 9. Against each name should be shown the overseas area in which the award was earned and the time spent therein.

(ii) Nominal rolls of V.A.D. members who did not enrol under the terms of A.C.I. **1778** of 1943 but who have qualified for the award under para. 2, should be submitted to the War Office (A.G. 4 Medals)) by the Secretary, V.A.D. Standing Committee. Against each name should be shown at least one qualifying establishment in which service was rendered and the dates of at least 28 days' qualifying service.

90. Deceased Personnel

Campaign stars and medals earned by members who have not lived to receive them will be given to the legal beneficiary of the deceased. The ribbon, however, will not be sent in advance, but will be issued with the Stars and Medals.

The completion of A.F. B 2070 and A.F. B 2068 will not normally be required, except when documents are not available, in which case the name and last recorded address of the legal beneficiary may be shown at Part I (3), the nature of the casualty at Part I (8) and details of issue will be recorded in the appropriate space on the reverse of the army form.

91. Home Guard

(i) **Instructions for Claiming Defence Medal**

(*a*) The administration of the award and issue of the Defence Medal to individuals who were enrolled in the Home Guard (formerly L.D.V.) and who completed the necessary qualifications during such service, should be undertaken by the County Territorial and Auxiliary Forces Associations. (In Northern Ireland by the Inspector General, Royal Ulster Constabulary, or the appropriate County Commandant, Ulster Special Constabulary.)

Where, however, an individual was subsequently commissioned or enlisted in the Army, the administration will be undertaken by the War Office, for officers and Records Offices for other ranks.

Service in a National Defence Company (formerly National Defence Corps), or in an Independent Local Defence Company, from or after 3rd September, 1939, may be aggregated with military service or Home Guard service or qualifying civilian service. Full details of such service will be shown on A.F. B 2068 (or when appropriate, on Civil Form D.M. 4).

(b) Ex-members of the Home Guard whose most recent qualifying service was rendered in the Home Guard, may obtain A.F. B 2068 from any Territorial and Auxiliary Forces Association H.Q. and after completion, it should be sent to the Association of the county in which service was last rendered. The National Registration number must be given on Part II of the form.

(ii) *Mixed Service*

(a) Enrolled Home Guard who subsequently enlisted in the Army, *but are not now serving*, may obtain A.F. B 2068 from any Territorial and Auxiliary Forces Association H.Q. or Records Office.

The claim forms should be sent by the individual to the appropriate Association H.Q. for completion of Part III and on its return, forward the form to the War Office, or appropriate Records Office. A list of Territorial and Auxiliary Forces Associations with the names and addresses is given in the Quarterly Army List.

(b) Those who have had previous qualifying service in the Royal Navy or Royal Marines and wish it to be aggregated with Home Guard service must show such service on A.F. B 2068, which should be forwarded to the Director of Accounts, Admiralty, for the completion of Part III and onward transmission of the claim to the Association H.Q. concerned.

(c) Ex-members of the Home Guard with previous qualifying service in the R.A.F. who wish it to be aggregated with qualifying Home Guard service, or other qualifying service, should show details of R.A.F. service on A.F. B 2068, which form should be forwarded to the Air Ministry (officers) or Air Officer i/c Records R.A.F., Gloucester, for completion of Part III and onward transmission to the Association H.Q. of the county in which the claimant last served.

(iii) (a) Those who rendered qualifying civilian service before becoming members of the Home Guard and wish to aggregate civilian service with Home Guard service should obtain a certificate on civil form D.M. 3 and attach it to A.F. B 2068 when sending the claim to the Territorial and Auxiliary Forces Association H.Q.

(b) Those who rendered qualifying civilian service after leaving the Home Guard and wish to aggregate Home Guard service with qualifying civilian service, should obtain a certificate on Civil Form D.M. 4 and attach it to Civil Form D.M. 2 when making a claim to the civil authority concerned.

A.F. B 2068 should *not* be used in these circumstances.

92. Disposal of Claim Forms

A.Fs. B 2068 should be kept in alphabetical collation until instructions have been given as to disposal.

93. Deceased Personnel

The Defence Medals earned by officers and other ranks of the Home Guard, who have not lived to receive them will be disposed of in accordance with King's Regulations, 1940, paragraph 1076.

The legal beneficiary of deceased Home Guard personnel may submit a claim to the Headquarters of the County Association concerned.

94. Foreign Subjects (Military)
Forms of Application and Declaration

(i) Foreign Nationals, commissioned or enlisted as individuals into the British Forces, who apply for the grant of campaign stars/medals, are required to complete A.F. B 2070/2068 and to attach thereto either a declaration as shown below, or a letter from their own government stating that the applicant is not eligible for and has not been granted an award equivalent to the British award(s) claimed.

DECLARATION

" I undertake, by my acceptance of a British award for my services with the British Armed Forces, that I shall not accept from my own Government, or any other Allied Government, a similar award, that is to say, any Allied Campaign Star or Medal instituted for the period for which the above awards have been granted (excluding any personal decorations or medal especially awarded to me).

I understand that the wearing of the ribbon of the British award will be invalidated by my acceptance of any other similar award as above defined ".

Signature ....

No. .... Rank .... Unit ....

Station .... Date ....

(ii) Foreign subjects eligible for campaign stars and medals should apply:—
  (a) if resident in the United Kingdom, to the War Office (officers) or to the Records Office (other ranks).
  (b) if in a British Colony, to the Colonial Secretary; or
  (c) if in any other country, to the nearest British Consul.

95. Instructions for Claiming Stars and Medals

(i) Polish officers and other ranks who served under British command, will be required to make a personal application for campaign stars and medals in the manner required for personnel of the British Armed Forces.

(ii) The claim form should be completed in accordance with the instructions on the form and in addition, should show the titles of both Polish and British units of formations with which service was rendered.

(iii) Serving personnel should submit their applications to the O.C. unit for action in accordance with para. 77. Claim Forms should be submitted to H.Q. Polish Resettlement Corps.

96. Civilian Qualifying Service in the United Kingdom—Defence Medal
Preamble

For the information of personnel overseas the procedure for claiming the Defence Medal on account of civilian qualifying service is given below and the list of the qualifying categories and the authority to whom the forms are to be sent are shown at Appendix D.

97. Civil Forms of Application

(i) Special forms for claiming the Defence Medal in respect of qualifying civilian service are available on request at the Home Office, Defence Medal Index, 59-67 Great Peter Street, S.W. 1 (or in the case of Scottish applicants, at Room 420, St. Andrew's House, Edinburgh 1).

(ii) (a) Civil Form D.M. 1 gives instructions relating to claims and at para. 15 is shown the categories (other than the Armed Forces) in the United Kingdom eligible to qualify for the award of the medal and the authorities to whom the claim should be sent.

(b) Civil Form D.M. 2 is a claim form and should be completed for the category in which the civilian claimant last served, or when a claim is to be made on behalf of a deceased person whose death occurred as a result of enemy action when on duty.

(c) Civil Form D.M. 3 should be completed when qualifying service in the category in which the claimant last served was less than three years and the claimant had had previous qualifying service in other categories with more than one authority or employer. (If the authority is the same for all periods of service, however, only Form D.M. 2 need be completed.) A separate Civil Form D.M. 3 will be required (except for the last period) for each period of service. The authority or authorities responsible for the earlier service will complete the certificate and the form should be attached to Civil Form D.M. 2 for aggregating the whole service.

Where certification is sought of the performance of fire guard or civil defence duty at business premises, Civil Form D.M. 3 should reach the local authority through the occupier of the business premises at which the services were rendered. The local authority should complete the form and return it to the applicant.

(d) Civil Form D.M. 4 is for use by ex-members of the armed forces (including the Home Guard) who rendered qualifying civilian service after retirement or discharge from the Service. (A.F. B 2068 will not be required.) When the form has been completed by the applicant, it should be sent to the Records Office or Service Department (officers) or the H.Qs. of the Territorial and Auxiliary Forces Association concerned, for certification. On its return, it should be attached to Civil Form D.M. 2 and both forms should then be sent to the authority for the *last* period of qualifying civilian service.

98. Instructions for Claiming the Defence Medal

(i) (a) If all the qualifying civilian service has been with one authority or employer, the completed Civil Form D.M. 2 should be sent to the authority for the service concerned, as shown in Appendix D.

(b) If qualifying service has been with more than one authority or employer, or a claim is made on behalf of a deceased person, whose death did not occur as a result of enemy action when on civilian duty, Civil Form D.M. 3 should be completed (except for the last period of service) and a certificate obtained from the appropriate authority or employer. On its return is should be attached to Civil Form D.M. 2 and both should be sent to the authority for the *last* period of service rendered as shown in Appendix D.

(c) Should Civil Form D.M. 2 be returned to the applicant undelivered, he should, if satisfied that it was correctly addressed, send it to the clerk of the local authority for the area in which qualifying service was rendered, attaching to it any civil forms D.M. 3 that may be required. A covering letter need not be sent as the post office marking will show that it was returned undelivered.

(ii) (*a*) When a claim is made for fireguard duties at business premises, the completed Civil Forms D.M. 2 or D.M. 3 should be sent to the employer at, or occupier of, those premises where service was rendered, for the certificate to be signed. The signatory should then send the form to the local government authorities, in whose area the service was rendered, or to the government department that acted as appropriate authority under the Fire Guard (Business and Government Premises) Order, 1943, for the completion of the certificate.

(*b*) If the form is not returned to the applicant within three months (six months for army personnel serving overseas), the applicant, if satisfied that it was correctly addressed, should then send a copy to the authority to whom the claims are to be sent (para. 15 of D.M. 1) explaining why this is being done.

(*c*) Should form D.M. 3 be returned to the applicant undelivered and he is satisfied that it was correctly addressed, it should be attached uncompleted to D.M. 2. The post office undelivered marking at the address space will show why the D.M. 3 was not completed.

(iii) (*a*) If civilian service was rendered after retirement or discharge from the forces, and it is desired to aggregate former military service with it, a certificate on Civil Form D.M. 4 should be obtained from the Records Office (other ranks) or War Office (officers) which is to be attached to form D.M. 2 when making a claim to the authorities concerned.

(*b*) If civilian service was rendered after Home Guard service and it is desired to aggregate it with the previous service, a certificate on Civil Form D.M. 4 should be obtained from the Headquarters of the Territorial and Auxiliary Forces Association of the county in which last served. On return it should be attached to form D.M. 2. when making a claim to the authorities concerned.

(iv)(*a*) Civilian foreign subjects should make applications as required for British civilians, on Civil Forms D.M. 2, D.M. 3 or D.M. 4.

(*b*) Foreign subjects whose last period of service was as a commissioned or enlisted member of the British Army will be required to complete A.F. B 2068 and to attach thereto D.M. 3 for any incomplete certified qualifying civilian service.

99. Deceased Personnel

The legal beneficiary of an individual whose death occurred as a result of enemy action when on duty, only need complete D.M. 2, but if death occurred otherwise, D.M. 3 will be required for incomplete service, and should be attached to D.M. 2, when forwarded to the authority concerned.

100. Colonial Civil Defence Organizations

Administration will be undertaken by the local government concerned and applications should be referred to the Colonial Office.

101. Annulment of Previous Instructions

A.C.I. **829** of 1945 and all War Office cables, memoranda and letters contrary to the revised instructions above are hereby superseded.

68/General 8533 (A.G. 4).

APPENDIX A

First Arakan Campaign—Qualifying Areas

(Referred to in para. 15 (iii))

The village of Dohazari and that part of Bengal which lies South of the following line—left bank of the R. Sangu from the sea to its junction with the Hunai Khiang (reference map sheet 84-C (1/253,440)) Assam-Bengal-Burma Point 4268, thence left bank of Hunai Khiang to stream junction at map reference Point 4966: thence due East to India-Burma border, together with the whole of the Arakan Division of Burma.

APPENDIX B

North-West Frontier of India—Qualifying Areas

(Referred to in para. 15 (iii))

Qualifying Areas, North-West Frontier.—Map references are to North-West Frontier series 1 inch to 1 mile.

(1) *Ahmedzai Wazir Salient, 3rd February, 1940, to 24th May, 1940.*

Area " A ".—From Midnight 2nd/3rd February, 1940, to Midnight 31st March/1st April, 1940.

Inclusive Thal to exclusive Kurram Muhammadzai inclusive road Kohat Bannu to inclusive Bannu exclusive road Bannu Pezu to exclusive Pezu exclusive road Pezu Tank to inclusive Tank to inclusive Manzai line of Administrative Border to inclusive Sherkhani to inclusive Khajuri Post to inclusive Mirali inclusive road Mirali Thal. The railway is exclusive throughout.

Area " B ".—From Midnight 31st March/1st April, 1940, to Midnight 15/16th April, 1940.

Inclusive Thal to exclusive Kurram Muhammadzai inclusive road Kohat Bannu to inclusive Bannu exclusive road Bannu Pezu to exclusive Pezu exclusive road Pezu Tank to inclusive Tank to inclusive Manzai line of Administrative Border to inclusive Sherkhani to inclusive Saidgi to inclusive Dattakhel 4781 to exclusive Shewa exclusive road Shewa Thal to inclusive Thal. The railway is exclusive throughout.

Area " C ".—From Midnight 15/16th April, 1940, to Midnight 30th April/1st May, 1940.

Inclusive Thal to exclusive Kurram Muhammadzai inclusive road Kohat Bannu to inclusive Bannu exclusive road Bannu Pezu to exclusive Pezu thence inclusive along the inter-district boundary between Bannu and D.I. Khan to where it meets the Administrative Border to inclusive Sherkhani to inclusive Saidgi to inclusive Dattakhel 4781 to exclusive Shewa exclusive road Shewa Thal to inclusive Thal. Railway is inclusive throughout.

Area " D ".—From Midnight 30th April/1st May, 1940, to Midnight 24th May, 1940.

Exclusive Thal to exclusive Kurram Muhammadzai inclusive road Kohat Bannu to inclusive Bannu exclusive road Bannu Pezu thence inclusive along the inter-district boundary between Bannu and Dera Ismail Khan District to where it meets the Administrative Border to inclusive Sherkani to inclusive Saidgi to inclusive Dattakhel 4781 to exclusive Shewa exclusive road Shewa Thal. The railway is exclusive throughout.

(2) *Tochi Valley, 18th June,* 1941, *to 26th August,* 1941.
From boundary pillar II (W 6274) along Durand Line to R. Kaitu (X 2594) along R. Kaitu to Spinwam Post (Z 4484) and to junction rivers Kaitu Kurram (Z 6084) thence South along River Kurram to Bannu thence to where R. Shaktu crosses Administrative Border (X 4439) to Madamir Kalai (X 1123) to Razmak then due west to boundary pillar XIV (W 4724) thence along Durand Line to boundary pillar II.

(3) *Datta Khel, 28th July,* 1942, *to 18th August,* 1942.
From boundary pillar II (W 6274) along Durand Line to R. Kaitu (X 2594) along R. Kaitu to Spinwam Post (Z 4484) and to junction rivers Kaitu Kurran (X 6084) thence South along River Kurran to Bannu thence to where R. Shaktu crosses Administrative Border (X 4439) to Madamir Kalai (X 1123) to Razmak thence due West to boundary pillar XIV (W 4724) thence along Durand Line to boundary pillar II.

APPENDIX C

Service in the undermentioned vessels, in support of operations in North Africa, during the period 23rd October, 1942 to 12th May, 1943, qualifies for the Clasp " North Africa 1942-43 ", under the conditions of paragraph 30 (vi).

Aba (H.M.H.S.)	Baron Jedburgh	City of Christchurch
Abbeydale (R.F.A.)(T)	Barrister	City of Christina
Adjutant	Bassethound	City of Edinburgh
Agatha (T)	Batory	City of Evansville
Aghios Nicolaos	Begum	City of Florence
Ah Kwang	Belgian Seamen (Bel)	City of Guildford
Ais Giorgis	Belray (Nor)	City of Keelung
Ajax	Benalbanach	City of Norwich
Akabahra	Benedict	City of Perth
Alcinous (Du)	Benledi	City of Pretoria
Alexandre Andre	Benrinnes	City of Rangoon
(T) (Bel)	Bergensfjord	City of Venice
Alisa (Pal)	Berto	City of Worcester
Alpera	Bjorkhaug (Nor)	Clan Lamont
Alphard (Du)	Blairnevis	Clan MacBean
Amra	Boissevain	Clan MacBrayne
Andes	Bolsta (Nor)	Clan Macindoe
Anglo African	Bretwalda	Clan Macinnes
Annitsa	Brinkburn	Clan MacTaggart
Antenor	Brittany Coast	Clan Murray
Antiklia (Gr)	Browning	Clausina (T)
Antonio	Brown Ranger	Cochrane
Antonio (T) (Du)	(R.F.A.) (T)	Collegian
Ardeola	Bruse Jarl (Nor)	Conakrian
Argos Hill	Bust (Nor)	Contractor
Armilla	Caithness	Coombehill
Arundel Castle	Calumet	Corona (Nor)
Ashantian	Cameronia	Corrales
Atlantic Coast	Carlton	Cowrie (T)
Audun (Nor)	Cathay	Coxwold
Aurora (Du)	Cefn-y-Bryn	Crista
Awatea	Cherryleaf (R.F.A.) (T)	Cromarty Firth
Baltonia	Christian Huygens	Cuba
Banfora	Circassia	Dafila
Bantria	City of Auckland	Dahomian

Daldorch
Dalhanna
Dalton Hall
Darien II (Pal)
Delane
Delilian
Dempe
Derbyshire
Derwentdale
      (R.F.A.) (T)
Derwent Hall
Destro
Dewdale (R.F.A.) (T)
Dingledale (R.F.A.)(T)
Director
Dorelian
Dorset Coast
Dorsetshire
Duchess of Bedford
Duchess of Richmond
Duchess of York
Duke of Athens
Dunnottar Castle
Durban Castle
Dux
Eastern City
Edencrag
Egret
Eildon
Elizabeth Bakke (Nor)
Elpis (Gr)
Empire Airman (T)
Empire Banner
Empire Baxter
Empire Beatrice
Empire Buckler
Empire Cabot
Empire Cameron
Empire Carpenter
Empire Centaur
Empire Chivalry
Empire Confidence
Empire Darwin
Empire Day
Empire Driver
Empire Dunstan
Empire Envoy
Empire Falcon
Empire Flamingo
Empire Foam
Empire Forest
Empire Gale
Empire Gat
Empire Cazelle
Empire Guinevere

Empire Harmony
Empire Haven
Empire Heath
Empire Heywood
Empire Hundter
Empire Kangaroo
Empire Lancer
Empire Lorenzo
Empire Mallory
Empire Mariott
Empire Metal
Empire Mordred
Empire Morn
Empire Nerissa
Empire Newton
Empire Nightingale
Empire Opossum
Empire Patrol
Empire Pride
Empire Prince
Empire Rhodes
Empire Rowan
Empire Ruskin
Empire Scout
Empire Shearwater
Empire Snipe
Empire Spinney
Empire Splendour
Empire Standard
Empire Summer
Empire Sunbeam
Empire Tern
Empire Torrent
Empire Webster
Empire Wordsworth
                (T)
Empire Wyclif
Empress of Australia
Empress of Canada
English Monarch
Ennerdale (R.F.A.)(T)
Esneh
Ettrick
Evvica
Explorer
Facto (Nor)
Fanad Head
Ferncliff (Nor)
Filleigh
Finira
Flora Nomikos (Gr)
Forest
Fort A. La. Corne
Fort Anne
Fort Augustus

Fort Babine
Fort Bourbon
Fort Chambly
Fort Chilcotin
Fort Confidence
Fort Douglas
Fort Ellice
Fort Gibraltar
Fort Halkett
Fort Lac La Ronge
Fort McLeod
Fort McLoughlin
Fort Norman
Fort Pitt
Fort Reliance
Fort Rupert
Fort St. James
Fort Senneville
Fort Simpson
Fort Steele
Fort Stikine
Fort Tadoussac
Fort Vermillion
Franconia
Frans Hals (Du)
Garlange
Genetor
Gibel Kebir
Glen Finlas
Gloucester
Govert Flink (Du)
Gudrun Maersk (Dan)
Hadleigh
Hampton Lodge
Hannah Moller
Harboe Jensen (Nor)
Harbury
Hardingham
Harmattan
Harpalyee
Harpalycus
Havildar
Hellas (Nor)
Heranger (Nor)
Hermelin
Hildur I
Hindustan
Hopecrown
Houston City
Imber
Indian Prince
Indra Poera
Inventor
·Intersum (Du)
Jacinth

Jade
Jean Jadot
Jenny Moller
Johan Van
    Oldenbarnevelt
June Crest
Kaimata
Kaipaki
Kalarand
Kaying
Kepong
Kingsland
Kisina
Kiung Chow
Kong Sverre (Nor)
Kroman (Pol)
Kwai Sang
Lagosian
Lalande
Lambrook
Lanarkshire
Leesang
Leopoldville
Letitia
Levern Bank
Lewant (Pol)
Liang Chow
Liberian
Linge
Livatho
Llandovery Castle
Llangibby Castle
Lochee
Lochmonar
Loriga
Lublin (Pol)
Lucijana (Y-S)
Lwow (Pol)
Lycaon
Lyeemon
Macharda
Mahout
Mahsud
Maine (H.M.H.S.)
Malayan Prince
Maloja
Mammy
Manchester Citizen
Manchester Commerce
Manchester Port
Marga
Marit Maersk (Gr)
Marnix Van
    St. Aldegonde
Maron

Mars (Du)
Mary Slessor
Masirah
Mausang
Melampus (Du)
Melmore Head
Merchant Prince
Meroe
Merope
Meta
Michalios
Middlesex Trader
Moanda (Bel)
Monarch of Bermuda
Mooltan
Moreton Bay
Mosna (Nor)
Myriel
Nairung
Narkunda
Narva
Nasprite (R.F.A.)
Nea Hellas
Nicoliaos G.
    Culucundis (Gr)
Nieuw Holland
Nieuw Zealand
Norelg
Norton
Novelist
Nur Jehan
Ocean Athlete
Ocean Courier
Ocean Fame
Ocean Freedom
Ocean Gallant
Ocean Liberty
Ocean Merchant
Re-named
    Jan Lievens (Du)
Ocean Messenger
Ocean Pilgrim
Ocean Rider
Ocean Seaman
Ocean Strength
Ocean Stranger
Ocean Trader
Ocean Traveller
Ocean Valentine
Ocean Vanity
Ocean Vanquisher
Ocean Vengeance
Ocean Verity
Ocean Veteran
Ocean Viceroy

Ocean Vigil
Ocean Virtue
Ocean Viscount
Ocean Vista
Ocean Volga
Ocean Voyager
Ocean Wanderer
Ocean Wayfarer
Odysseus (Du)
Ophalia
Orbita
Orient City
Orion
Ormonde
Orontes
Orpheus
Otranto
Ousel
Pacific Exporter
Pacific Grove
Pacific Shipper
Pahang
Palermo
Palima (Du)
Panama
Pardo
Penshurst
Peri Bonka
Petrella (R.F.A.)
P.L.M. 21
Polo
Popi (Gr)
Portsea
Port St. John
Prince de Liege
Princess Kathleen
Prometheus
Promise (Nor)
Pronto
Rajput
Rallus
Rangitata
Rangitiki
Recorder
Reina Del Pacifico
Robert Maersk
Romney
Rossum (Du)
Rudby
Runo
Saint Bernard
St. Clears
St. Essylt
St. Merriel
Salacia

Salter's Gate
Samaria
San Amando (T)
Sapa Roea (Du)
Scythia
Seapool
Selbo (Nor)
Selvik
Serula
Shoreham
Shuna
Sicilian Prince
Silver Laurel
Sobieski
Sobo
Sofala
Sophie
Spero
Stad Haarlem (Du)
Stad Maasluis (Du)
Staffordshire
Stancleeve
Stanhill
Star
Stirling Castle
Stirlingville (Nor)

Strathaird
Strathallan
Stratheden
Strathmore
Strathnaver
Sui Yang
Suncrest
Sutherland
Switzerland
Tadorna
Taiposhan
Tamarao
Tarantia
Tawali (Du)
Tegelberg
Temple Inn
Theseus
Thistledale
Thurland Castle
Tiba (Du)
Titus (Du)
Topdalsjford (Nor)
Torfinnjarl (Nor)
Toronto (Nor)
Torr Head
Trader

Trajanus (Du)
Trent Bank
Triona
Troubadour (Nor)
Tureby (Dan)
Turkistan
Tynemouth
Urlana
Vanellus
Varvara
Vasco
Viceroy of India
Ville D'Anvers
Ville de Strasbourg
Volendam
Volsella
Warwick Castle
Wearpool
Welsh Trader
West Point
Winchester Castle
Windsor Castle
Zaan (Du)
Zena

KEY

Bel	Belgian
Dan	Danish
Du	Dutch
Gr	Greek
Nor	Norwegian
Pal	Palestinian
Pol	Polish
Y-S	Yugoslav
H.M.H.S.	H.M. Hospital Ship
R.F.A.	Royal Fleet Auxiliary
T	Tanker

APPENDIX D

Categories (other than serving members of the armed forces or the Women's Auxiliary Services) in the United Kingdom eligible for the award of the Defence Medal and addresses to which claims should be sent.

Category No. *Category and address for claims*

1. Ex-members of the Armed forces or of the Women's Military Auxiliary Services.
2. Home Guard.—Send claims to the appropriate Territorial and Auxiliary Forces County Association. (In the case of the Ulster Home Guard, the Inspector-General, Royal Ulster Constabulary, or the appropriate County Commandant, Ulster Special Constabulary.)

Category No.	Category and address for claims
3	Civil Defence Warden Service (including Shelter Wardens).—Send claims to the clerk of the local authority with which the service was given, or in the case of service given in the London deep tube shelters, to the Home Office, Whitehall, S.W.1.
4	Civil Defence Rescue Service (including former First Aid Party Service, or in London, Stretcher Party Service).—Send claims to the clerk of the local authority with which the service was given.
5	Civil Defence Decontamination Service.—Send claims to the clerk of the local authority with which the service was given.
6	Civil Defence Report and Control Service.—Send claims to the clerk of the local authority with which the service was given.
7	Civil Defence Messenger Service.—Send claims to the clerk of the local authority with which the service was given.
8	Civil Defence Ambulance Service (including Sitting Case Cars).—Send claims to the clerk of the local authority with which the service was given.
9	Civil Defence First Aid Service (including first aid posts and points, public cleansing centres, mobile cleansing units and the nursing service for public air raid shelters).—Send claims to the clerk of the local authority with which the service was given, or, in the case of service given in the London deep tube shelters, to the Home Office, Whitehall, S.W.1.
10	Civil Defence Gas Identification Service.—Send claims to the clerk of the local authority with which the service was given.
11	Rest Centre Service.—Send claims to the clerk of the local authority with which the service was given:—of para. 61 (iii) (*d*).
12	Emergency Food Service (including Queen's Messenger Convoy Service).—Send claims to the clerk of the local authority with which the service was given:—of para. 61 (iii) (*d*).
13	Canteen Service.—Send claims to the clerk of the local authority with which the service was given:—of para. 61 (iii) (*d*).
14	Administrative and Information Centre Service (not Ministry of Information service—*see* category (43)).—Send claims to the clerk of the local authority with which the service was given.
15	Mortuary Service.—Send claims to the clerk of the local authority with which the service was given.
16	Fire guards who performed duties under a local authority.—Send claims to the clerk of the local authority with which the service was given.
17	Fire guards (including civil defence and fire brigade personnel) who performed duties at government or business premises.—Send claims to the head of the establishment at government premises or the occupier at business premises at which the duties were performed. In the case of duties performed in the City of London at business premises other than than those at which the applicant was employed, claims should be sent to the Town Clerk, Corporation of London, 55-61, Moorgate, London, E.C.1.
18	Women's Voluntary Services for Civil Defence.—Send claims to the W.V.S. Centre Organizer.

Category No.	Category and address for claims
19.	Civil Nursing Reserve (Applications in respect of service in the Civil Defence First-Aid Service should be made as laid down for category (9)).—Send claims to the employing authority with which the service was given.
20	Nurses or Midwives in hospitals for which government departments or local authorities are responsible, or in the recognized voluntary hospitals.—Send claims to the superintendent or secretary of the hospital in which the service was given.
21	National Fire Service (including service in a local authority fire brigade or the Auxiliary Fire Service before nationalization).—Send claims to the nearest fire station. (In the case of the National Fire Service (Northern Ireland), the Establishment Officer, Ministry of Home Affairs, Stormont, Belfast.)
22	Police (Regular Police, First Police Reserve, Police War Reserve, Women's Auxiliary Police Corps, Police Auxiliary Messenger Service, Special Constabulary).—Send claims to the chief officer of police concerned. (In the case of the Ulster Special Constabulary, the appropriate County or City Commandant.)
23	Royal Marine Police Special Reserve.—Send claims to the Chief Constable, Royal Marine and Admiralty Civil Police, through head of establishment where duty was performed.
24	Admiralty Civil Police.—Send claims to the Chief Constable, Royal Marine and Admiralty Civil Police, through head of establishment where duty was performed.
25	War Department Constabulary.—Send claims to the Chief Constable, War Department Constabulary, War Office, London, S.W. 1.
26	Air Ministry Constabulary.—Send Claims to the Under-Secretary of State, Air Ministry (S. 5 (d)), Bush House, N.W. Wing, W.C. 2, through head of establishment where the duty was performed.
27	Railway and Dock Police.—Send claims to the chief officer of police of the railway or dock authority concerned.
28	Civil Defence Services set up by railway, dock authority and canal undertakings.—Send claims to the appropriate undertaking concerned.
29	American Ambulance, Great Britain.—Send claims to the Ministry of Health, Whitehall, London, S.W. 1.
30	Civil Air Transport (Air crew only).—Send claims to the Ministry of Civil Aviation, Ariel House C.H. 8 (c)), Strand, W.C.2.
31	Air Transport Auxiliary (Air crew only).—Send claims to the Ministry of Supply and Aircraft Production, Millbank, S.W. 1.
32	Civil Defence Reserve.—Send claims to the Home Office, Whitehall, London, S.W. 1.
33	Kent County Civil Defence Mobile Reserve.—Send claims to the Clerk of the Kent County Council, Maidstone, Kent.
34	West Sussex County Civil Defence Mobile Reserve.—Send claims to the Clerk of the West Sussex County Council, Chichester, Sussex.
35	Coast Guards.—Send claims to the Principal Establishment Officer, Ministry of War Transport, Berkeley Square House, London, W. 1.

Category No.	Category and address for claims
36	Civil Servants forming departmental Civil Defence organizations.—Send claims to the departmental headquarters or head of the local establishment concerned.
37	Lighthouse Keepers who served under the three general lighthouse authorities, and keepers of light vessels under those authorities, who do not qualify for the 1939-45 Star.—Send claims to the general lighthouse authority concerned.
38	Port of London Authority River Emergency Service.—Send claims to the General Manager, Port of London Authority, Trinity Square, London, E.C.3.
39	Clyde River Patrol.—Send claims to the Flag Officer-in-Charge, St. Enoch's Hotel, Glasgow.
40	Royal Observer Corps.—Send claims to the Royal Observer Corps, Area Headquarters of the area in which the applicant served.
41	Volunteer Stretcher Bearers (Emergency Hospital Scheme).—In England, Wales and Northern Ireland send claims to the superintendent of the hospital concerned. In Scotland, to the Department of Health for Scotland, St. Andrew's House, Edinburgh 1.
42	Male Orderlies in Casualty Evacuation Trains (Emergency Medical Service).—In England and Wales send claims to the Ministry of Health, Whitehall, London, S.W.1. In Scotland, to the Department of Health for Scotland, St. Andrew's House, Edinburgh, 1. In Northern Ireland, to the Ministry of Health and Local Government, Stormont, Belfast.
43	Emergency Information Officers and their helpers (who served under the Ministry of Information, and including deputy E.I.Os., announcers, drivers and messengers, if engaged in a section of the service which had, or would have had, operational functions during or immediately after enemy attacks).—Send claims to the Regional Information Officer (Ministry of Information) for the Civil Defence Region in which the claimant served.
44	R.A.F. Education Officers serving in the United Kingdom.—Send claims to the Under-Secretary of State, Air Ministry (E.S. 1), Alexandra House, Kingsway, W.C.2.
45	Enrolled Lifeboatmen (R.N.L.I.) who do not qualify for the 1939-45 Star.—Send claims to the Secretary, Royal National Lifeboat Institution, Boreham Wood, Elstree, Herts.
46	Lloyds Signal Stations in the United Kingdom.
47	Departmental Civil Defence Organizations.

REGIMENTAL HISTORIES OF THE BRITISH ARMY

A SELECTION OF N&MP REPRINTED TITLES
ALWAYS AVAILABLE ALWAYS IN PRINT

Read the real history of The Second World War in the stories of the Regiments, Corps, Divisions, & Battalions that fought it.

NAVAL & MILITARY PRESS
WWW.NAVAL-MILITARY-PRESS.COM

CLUB ROUTE IN EUROPE
The Story of 30 Corps in the European Campaign.
9781783311033

30 Corps was heavily involved in the closing campaigns of the Second World War in Europe, starting when its 50th (Northumbrian) Division landed on Gold Beach on D-day. It helped to clear the Cotentin peninsular in Operation Bluecoat and, after General Brian Horrocks took over command, it took part in Operation Market Garden at Arnhem, and the crossing of the Rhine into the German heartland. A superb unit history of these often difficult and bloody operations.

SEVENTH ARMOURED DIVISION
October 1938 - May 1943
9781474539180

2nd BATTALION SOUTH WALES BORDERS 24th REGIMENT
D-DAY TO VE-DAY
9781474539012

Describing the campaign from D-Day onwards, this excellent contemporary battalion history is divided into two parts. The first contains an outline of the activities of the 2/24th during the campaign in Europe from D-Day to VE-Day, and the second is a detailed narrative of some of the more important actions in which the battalion fought. Complete with a list of awards. Originally printed in Hamburg in 1945.

49 (WEST RIDING) RECONNAISSANCE REGIMENT
Royal Armoured Corps - Summary of Operations June 1944 to May 1945
9781474536677

Rare Reconnaissance unit history that was completed immediately after the war had ended. Following the D-Day invasions, the 49th Reconnaissance Regiment fought as Montgomery's left flank, and played vital roles in the capture of Arnhem, and the liberation of Holland. They are honoured annually in Utrecht to this day. The book is completed with 2 good coloured maps.

THE HISTORY OF THE CORPS OF ROYAL MILITARY POLICE
9781783310951

Excellent history of this corps, almost entirely devoted to WW2 on all fronts, including Middle East, North-West Europe and Burma. Complete with a Roll of Honour.

THE STORY OF THE 79th ARMOURED DIVISION OCTOBER 1942 - JUNE 1945
9781783310395

A magnificent and fully illustrated official history of Britain's 79th Armoured Division - the specialised unit which developed and operated 'Hobart's Funnies', the adapted tanks which carried out a range of tasks on D-day and after ranging from mine clearance to bridge laying. Follows the unit from its formation to victory in Europe.

HISTORY OF THE ARGYLL & SUTHERLAND HIGHLANDERS 7th BATTALION
From El Alamein To Germany
9781781519653

THE ESSEX REGIMENT 1929 - 1950
9781781519813

Comprehensive history of both regular & territorial force battalions, mainly Middle East (inc. Tobruk & Alamein), North-West Europe & 1st Bn. with Chindits in Burma 1944. Rolls of Honour and awards.

HISTORY OF THE IRISH GUARDS IN THE SECOND WORLD WAR
9781474537094

A fine history of a proud regiment; The Irish Guards played their part gallantly during campaigns in Europe, North Africa and Italy during the Second World War, claiming two Victoria Cross recipients during that conflict. The basis of this history was the War Diaries kept by Battalion Intelligence Officers, along with individual records and papers. A Roll of Honour, Honours Awards down to Military Medal, and 22 good maps complete this very good WW2 Regimental.

ALGIERS TO AUSTRIA
The 78th Division in the Second World War
9781783310265

OPERATIONS OF THE EIGHTH CORPS
The River Rhine to the Baltic Sea. A narrative account of the pursuit and final defeat of the German Armed Forces March-May 1945.
9781474538176

THE HISTORY OF THE 51st HIGHLAND DIVISION 1939-1945
9781474536660

The 51st Highland Division fought and lost in France in 1940, was reborn, and fought and won in the North African desert, Sicily and finally in North Western Europe from D-Day to the end of the war. As a division the men earned the respect of friend and foe alike, and this is their story. Amply illustrated with 36 photographs, 18 maps and battle plans (many coloured) that help the reader to follow the course of the conflict. A good index (persons, units and place names) and a statistical battle casualties list complete this good WW2 Divisional History

THE HISTORY OF THE FIFTEENTH SCOTTISH DIVISION 1939-1945
9781783310852

Formed at the outbreak of war in September 1939, the 15th (Scottish) division served in North-western Europe after landing in Normandy soon after D-day on 14 June 1944. It fought on the Odon River, at Caen, Caumont, Mont Pincon, the Nederrijn, the Rhineland, and across the Rhine. On April 10, 1946, the division was disbanded. The total number of casualties it sustained during the 12 months of fighting was 11,772.

THE STORY OF THE ROYAL ARMY SERVICE CORPS, 1939-1945
9781474538251

A complete history of the RASC in all theatres throughout the Second World War. This a model unit history originally published under the direction of the Institution of the Royal Army Service Corps, it is excellently produced, and arranged by theatre of war. The narrative is full with technical information, and the many photographic plates record visually British military vehicles in service situations.

www.ingramcontent.com/pod-product-compliance
Lightning Source LLC
LaVergne TN
LVHW021619080426
835510LV00019B/2666